Debbie G

ANNE GOODALL

IT IS NEVER TOO LATE

Amazing Life After Death Communications

TRIAD

© Copyright 1996 by Anne Goodall

All rights reserved under International and Pan-American Copyright Conventions.

No part of this book may be reproduced or transmitted in any form, by any means, electronic or mechanical, including photocopying or recording or by any information storage or retrieval system, without express permission in writing from the publisher.

For information address: TRIAD Publishers Pty. Ltd.
P.O. Box 731, Cairns, Qld. 4870, Australia

Book title: It Is Never Too Late
Author: Anne Goodall
Cover art: Hartmut Jäger
National Library of Australia: ISBN: 0 9586707 1 4
Printed in Australia

International Distributors:

Australia: Gemcraft Books, 14 Duffy St., Burwood, Vic. 3125
Ph: (03) 98880111 Fax: (03) 98880044

New Zealand: Peaceful Living Publications, P.O. Box 300, Tauranga, N.Z. Ph: (07) 571 8105 Fax: (07) 571 8513

U.K: Gazelle Book Services Ltd., Falcon House, Queen Square, Lancaster LA1 1RN, England. Ph: (1524) 68765 Fax: (1524) 63232

USA: New Leaf Distributing, 401 Thornton Rd.,Lithia Springs, GA 30057-1557, USA, Ph: (770) 948 7845 Fax: (770) 944 2813

*Triad publications aim at aiding and inspiring
a spiritually unfolding humanity.*

Acknowledgments

A special thank you to Marion, who gave so much help and support to Mark from his first illness to the time of his death, and also gave me the confidence to continue with the communications.

My sincere thanks to Lucy, whose enthusiasm and interest encouraged me to begin to collate the messages I had received so that they might benefit others. And to Elizabeth, who encouraged me with her support and optimism and gave unstintingly of her time, as she patiently listened, edited and tidied up my own writing.

With perfect timing Felicity then appeared and, through her understanding of the concepts expressed in the book, was able to assist with the preparation of the final manuscript. My gratitude to her.

WHAT IS DYING?

A ship sails and I stand - watching till she
fades on the horizon and someone
at my side says, 'she is gone'.
Gone where? Gone from my sight, that is all;
she is just as large as when I saw her. The
diminished size and total loss of sight is in
me, not in her, and just at the moment when
someone at my side says 'She is gone',
there are others who are watching her
coming, and other voices take up a glad
shout, 'There she comes!' -
and that is dying.

Bishop Brent

CONTENTS

Chapter I
My Life 7
The Writing 29

Chapter II
The Communications Begin 35
Early Experiences And Learning 51
Recalling With Regret 63
The White Light And Auras 68
On Prayer 74
Prayers For The Departed 84

Chapter III
Masks 89
Spiritual Healing 92
Health 94
Our Ideas Of Self 97
Where Is The World Going? 99
Destiny And Free Will 101
Giving To Self 107
Money 108
Channeling Or Mediumship 111
Temper 116
Expectations 118

Chapter III Continued

Perception And Interpretation *122*
Right And Wrong *125*
Scientific Breakthroughs *127*
Meditation *129*
Illusion *130*
The Way People View Their Lives *131*
Power Of Thoughts *133*
When Two Loves Are Waiting, What Then? ... *134*
Mark's Conclusion *136*
My Conclusion *140*

Introduction

I have chosen to write this book under a pseudonym in order to protect those who were part of the events but who may not wish to be seen to have been involved. For this reason I have changed the names of the principal characters and also some of the minor details. Nevertheless, the outline of my life prior to the main part of the book is basically as it happened and the changes in the way I saw things then and how I see them now are a reality.

I had read about people who had received, by a number of varying means, what were called 'communications from the other side'. These communications give evidence that the soul survives death. They show that when the physical body dies the soul or spirit continues on into another realm or dimension. In rare and special circumstances, this energy can make contact with a family member or friend through someone who is still living. The person through whom the communication is made is called a 'channel' or a 'medium'.

Mark and I were married for forty years. The fact that our life together was not particularly out of the ordinary adds significance to the way things eventually worked out. Throughout our married life there was not one occasion when he gave either me or our children any reason to think that he believed in anything of a spiritual or metaphysical nature. In fact I recall one occasion, early on, when he professed to

Introduction

being an agnostic. This book is about our life together insofar as it relates to the many communications I received from him after his death. These communications told me about his experience of death and included much information of a spiritual, family and personal nature. They shared with me some aspects of his own spiritual growth and other experiences he has had since he passed from this earthly existence.

In view of how I perceived our marriage, and from what I thought I knew of my husband's values while we were married, the communications were as unexpected as were their contents. They were all the more remarkable if one considers that we did not experience any closeness on any level during the forty years of our marriage. At first I found the communications extremely difficult to accept and I could not bring myself to tell anyone about them for a long time.

After many months, and as a result of these communications, I realised how much my understanding of the meaning of death had expanded. My whole outlook on life, and especially my feelings about our life together, had become something incredible and wonderful; all the pain had been resolved. I began to wonder if my experience, which had provided me with such inspiration, could be of equal help to others. The enthusiasm of two friends in whom I finally confided, together with the support of Mark and his loving teachers on the other side, encouraged me to start collating the wealth of information I had received.

I believe that there are many people who have lost

Introduction

a loved one who are not able to come to terms with their feelings of regret, anger, resentment or guilt. I dedicate this book to them. I hope that it may help them to realise it is never too late to ask for forgiveness and understanding, no matter how difficult the event or situation appears to have been, or how painful the memories. To quote Mark, this book will '*help sorrowing people who are full of regrets for what they did or had done to them; or for words said or left unspoken*'.

Chapter I

My Life

I chose as my parents a handsome man and a beautiful woman. The only attributes I believed I had inherited were good health, good skin, curly hair and a firm chin. I once read that an only child can either be the total focus of its parents, and become very spoilt and undisciplined, or it can feel like a dwarf in the land of giants. I remember I did feel very small so the latter described exactly how I felt.

I never doubted that I was loved, but I suspected (quite mistakenly I am sure) that it was conditional upon my behaviour. In any case, I knew I had to be good and obedient; any defiantly expressed disagreement on my part resulted in an instant reaction from my mother. I can still hear her saying reproachfully, 'Oh Anne, back answering like that is an absolute sin'.

Our lives were governed by what our church taught. My father said prayers for us before and after meals. A lengthy devotional reading followed dinner in the evening. From an early age I thought it strange that our church was the *only* church that taught the Word of God in its truth and purity - with the implication that we were the only ones, presumably, who would be saved and go to heaven. It became quite a worry to me when I learnt what the dire alternative was; especially when I realised that my classmates and their families had almost no chance of spending eternity in heavenly bliss with me. On the contrary, they had every chance of being very uncomfortable indeed.

It Is Never Too Late - Chapter 1

I realised deep down, in spite of our church's teaching, that if God was a God of love, if He was all powerful, all knowing and in charge of everything, He would not arrange for all the people in the rest of the world to be born into situations where they would never be able to hear about His Son, much less become members of our church. I could not believe that He would exclude countless millions and more of His beloved children from His Kingdom; I was sure that He would make other arrangements for them.

My father conducted his business from home which gave him the flexibility to arrange his own working hours. As an Elder of the church he took his responsibilities very seriously. This meant regular attendance at all church services, including the funerals whenever possible. My mother, who was one of the organists, always accompanied him. So did I, until I started school. How well I remember walking up the aisle with the rest of the mourners and peering into the coffin through the fine transparent veil which was always draped so artistically over the top. Even now I cannot smell the strong perfume of a particular flower without immediately seeing someone's dearly beloved reclining peacefully on white satin. These experiences may have been what kindled an intense interest for me in things that go bump in the night.

I could not help but wonder at this early age what really happened at death. What was the process called dying? It puzzled me why death was always spoken of as a tragedy - something which was apparently to be feared and avoided at all costs. I wondered what there was to fear if, as the church taught, our whole life was devoted to making us more worthy and acceptable to God and life in eternity with Him.

The years passed rapidly. I continued to puzzle inconclusively over many similar issues from time to time and often felt drawn to reading articles on subjects which I knew were frowned upon by our church. Our minister was a sincere and kind man who took his chosen calling with utmost seriousness. Unfortunately, I did not feel that I could confide in him and express my doubts about the increasing incompatibility of the way I saw some things and the stance that our church took.

At the age of eighteen I left school and found myself a job. Among the many new people I came into contact with was a man called Bob. One day he casually talked about how he had first met his wife. He had seen the face of a beautiful young woman in a gypsy's crystal ball and the gypsy told him that she was the woman he would marry. The prediction did come true even though it was not until ten years later. Bob finished his romantic story by adding that they had been together many times before. In that instant I felt that I had found a missing link in the puzzle of life - another piece of the jigsaw had been put into place. A world of new possibilities had suddenly opened up for me. Was it really possible that this is not the only life we have to live?

During the months that followed, Bob and I shared

many absorbing discussions. I began searching out information about so many fascinating things - the existence of auras, near-death experiences, the possibility of communications from the other side through mediums and the reality of nature spirits I had previously thought were childish fantasies. The list went on.

The theory of reincarnation had a particularly transforming effect on me. It shed some light on the seeming injustices and inequalities in the world. I had always been troubled by what appeared to be inexplicable tragedies and horrors which occurred regularly in the world, even though I had been brought up with glib statements which assured me that it was not right for us to question God's will.

Dancing was among the numerous pleasures not condoned by our church. This was one rule I found very difficult to accept. In fact, I spent my childhood and early teens feeling rebellious about what I saw as a deprivation. The preparations for the annual school ball held particularly dark memories for me for many years. Almost the entire school had taken part in practising the grand march every year in the school grounds while I had to watch from the apparent safety of an upstairs window. I could not work out why it was considered so sinful to attend a function where children simply marched around in their fancy dress and had fun.

During the war, young service personnel chose to attend our church's services. At last there was no lack of social activity. My life suddenly brightened up with the closer proximity of so many young men! They were invited to the homes, cared for at the church canteen and included in group outings. It was then that I met David, an Englishman, who was stationed nearby. We experienced an instant mutual attraction, leading quickly and inexorably to a deep love. It was sheer magic.

There were so many boys who were members of our church to whom I could have been attracted, and yet I had to meet and fall in love with the only son of a clergyman of another denomination. My father began to question David's beliefs as soon as he realised that here was a potential suitor. David was reluctant to consider changing his own particular faith, and as a result we were forbidden to even think of making plans for the future. What were we going to do now? How could we suddenly switch off the magic of our love and ignore the depth of our feelings? So, despite such strong parental disapproval, we continued our precious relationship. David and I planned to marry as soon as I turned twenty-one. We had decided that he would either return for the marriage, or I would join him in England if my parents had not relented by then.

When David was transferred to another base overseas a few months later, we wrote to each other every day. He sent most of his letters to my work address, with only the occasional one home, in an attempt to minimise the on-going parental opposition. My father told me many times that when David returned home he would forget me. Meanwhile, I continued to dream about our future together.

The war ended and David returned home. Immediately his letters became shorter, less frequent and without any mention of our future. It seemed as though my father had been right. After some time of anguish, and what had obviously become vain hope, I released David in a brief letter. He sent me a short, regretful answer which suggested that we had to accept this as being God's will. I well remember how angrily and sadly I thought that this was yet another thing in my life which I did not believe was God's will!

After my father's death some years later, I found copies of his letters to David's father, and the replies meticulously filed. It was only then that I realised why the dreams David and I had dared to dream remained unfulfilled - we had not counted on the strength of the opposition of the two fathers, each as unyielding and authoritarian as the other. My mother appeared at the time to have agreed wholeheartedly with my father, but many years later she confided in me that she believed David and I would have been perfect for each other. She said she had felt it was wrong of my father to stand in the way of our happiness and would always regret not having opposed him.

The light and joy had gone from my life. The future looked bleak. My social life consisted of indifferent tennis with the church group, and the Youth Bible Study once a fortnight. Even square dancing was forbidden. I could see a long, dreary spinsterhood ahead of me, of work and church activities. Then Mark came into my life.

My father's business was flourishing. Mark was among the young men sometimes brought in to help after hours and dinner with the family was often included. He was tall, dark and good-looking. He was also quiet and well-mannered, and my father was impressed by his ability and his willingness to work hard. Mark asked my father's permission to take me out. We went to movies and concerts and I was relieved that he did not care about dancing. After a few months Mark broached the question of marriage. Because of the last bitter experience, I had resolved *never* to go against my father again. To my surprise, Mark was willing to take a lengthy course of instruction from our minister, and joined our church. It seemed that this time my hopes for a happier future would eventuate.

I had realised that Mark was an uncommunicative man, but I had no problem compensating for his silence! In hindsight, I agree with my father who once commented that it is difficult to get to know someone if they never speak! Later I realised that what I took to be Mark's silent approval of my happy chattering about how our future life would be was no such thing. Because he shared so little of himself with me, I never really knew what he was thinking or what he thought married life should be like.

It took only four days into our marriage to discover what Mark felt were the roles of husbands and wives in respect to so-called housework. We were staying at

It Is Never Too Late - Chapter 1

a guesthouse and shared a table with two other couples married on the same day that we were. In a general discussion at breakfast it was decided that the laundry needed to be done before our usual morning swim.

When the others had finished in the laundry I told Mark we could now do our washing. He did not jump to his feet, but continued reading. Thinking he had not heard, I made the announcement even more clearly. He came with me and it was obvious he had never washed anything in his life. I suggested that I wash and he rinse and wring out. Mark stood silently as I rubbed away, and then asked, 'What is that?', pointing to a huge mangle standing in the corner. I said it was probably used for the guesthouse linen. Mark said, 'Well, why can't we use that instead of doing it by hand?' I said I thought it would be harder to move those huge rollers than to wring the clothes by hand and, besides, you could not put anything through with buttons on as they would break off.

Mark picked up a pair of his shorts, looked at me, and to my astonishment fed them through the huge tight rollers of the mangle. He managed to break off every button on the fly and the waistband, then put the shorts in the basket and walked out of the laundry. There was no discussion about the incident but the message was clear. Mark did not, then or ever, consider that helping a wife with domestic chores was part of a husband's role.

In spite of the restrictions of my home life, where there had never been anything remotely resembling a frank question and answer session on sex, I managed to develop a healthy interest in the subject! I read an informative book about the mechanics of sex, and took part in countless fascinating discussions on the subject with friends. My fertile imagination supplied the magic and bliss of how it would be when my turn came. I felt sure that any lack of romance in my relationship with Mark would change once we were married.

It was exciting, for a short time - until I realised that the warmth and intimacy we shared in the bedroom would not ever extend into our everyday lives. The marriage, which had given me some hope of happiness, soon became a disaster for me. Any ideas that I had had of love, companionship and support quickly disappeared. With no love or affection shown outside the bedroom, my enthusiasm for the physical part of our marriage declined rapidly. I began to long for some sign of caring, no matter how slight. A kiss for no reason at all would have been wonderful. A perfunctory peck on my cheek as Mark left the house in the morning seemed to be my ration.

I found it impossible to express my dissatisfaction with things of a deeply personal nature, but I was not backward in voicing my disapproval and disappointment in areas of less importance. But eventually I realised how pointless it was. Mark totally ignored what I was saying and I became more upset at having been ignored! Better not to have mentioned it in the first place. If I repeated a request because it had been ignored, I was told angrily that I was *always* nagging. I decided that the thing to do was to calmly and sensibly talk it out with Mark and not to wait until my frustration caused me to speak without thinking (which had never brought results).

After much thought and mental rehearsal, I told Mark I would like to speak to him about something important and I would like him to hear me out. I expressed my disappointments, told him how I wished things were, explained the areas I found so difficult to accept, and so on. In conclusion I said that I knew that he must find things that I said and did or didn't do equally frustrating and upsetting and I really wanted him to tell me so I could try to do better. Mark looked at me with his cold eyes and expressionless face and said, 'You don't know you're alive, that's your trouble', and walked to his car and drove off.

In the back of my mind, as each child arrived, I sustained the vague, undefined hope that maybe now it would be different. Nothing changed of course. We began to lead separate lives; Mark loved his work and I was kept busy with the home, the children and all that that entailed. I had such strong ideas of how a husband should be, how he should behave towards his wife and family, and what a wife's role was. I can now see how unrealistic these ideals were; they did not in any way match my daily existence. Mark and I did not even share a similar sense of humour.

As a result of what seemed to be Mark's stern and strict moral values, I learned to temper my lighthearted

It Is Never Too Late - Chapter 1

and overly broad-minded comments on life in general.

Mark was brilliant at his work. It was not long before he was offered a position at a much higher salary. This new position involved travel and kept him away a great deal. Even when he was home he frequently worked late at the office. I had never been aware of being a lonely only child, but I experienced loneliness at a deep level once I was married, in spite of a comfortable home, security and healthy, intelligent children.

It was not long before I started to blame myself for the situation. Any lack in our relationship had surely to be my fault, I thought. Obviously I did not come up to Mark's standards. Had I possessed the right qualities, whatever they were, things would have been better. And surely the fact that I had not loved Mark as I had loved David, was also to blame. After Mark and I announced our engagement, my mother unexpectedly asked me 'What would you do if David came back?' I can still hear my unhesitating reply: 'Well, if I were walking down the aisle to marry Mark and I saw David, and I knew he still wanted me, I would turn around and leave with him.'

Those words often haunted me. How terribly wrong it had been for me to marry Mark, realising our marriage would not have the quality of what I had expected to experience with David.

My perception of Mark was that he had so little in his life - only his work really. Surely he must long for a loving relationship?

I began to pray that he would meet someone who could bring the warmth and joy into his life that I had been unable to give him.

After some years of marriage, and at my lowest ebb, I thought that a marriage guidance counsellor might be able to help me. The counsellor offered me two possibilities. He said that as far as he could surmise, my husband was motivated totally by ambition and would be unlikely to change. Therefore I could leave, or stay and make an independent life for myself. I had never considered that leaving was an option, and I had already made my own life, such as it was, so things continued as before.

Perhaps it was all the anguish and inner conflict that I was going through which pushed me to search even more earnestly for spiritual truths. I chanced to come across a remarkable book, *Edgar Cayce: Man of Miracles*. Cayce was an American, a devout Christian and a student of the Bible, and his story particularly appealed to me. He discovered that while in a trance he could not only diagnose illnesses but could see the cause and prescribe the remedy or treatments required. The main difference between his gift and other comparably powerful mystics and psychics was that almost all of his readings (some fourteen thousand) were faithfully recorded, and remain available to anyone to peruse, with the Association for Research and Enlightenment (A.R.E.) at Virginia Beach, Virginia.

I decided to join the Association. Through their numerous publications, which were available to the public, I was able to continue my searching and widen my knowledge.

Books on spiritual development, meditation, self-awareness, psychic phenomena, reincarnation and so on were not as prolific then as they are now. I considered myself fortunate to come across such a wealth of study material to further feed my insatiable appetite for knowledge, and answer more of my long-standing questions. Mark was not interested in any of the books I read, or the beliefs I held so dear - just as politics and sport held no interest for me.

So I soon found myself leading a double life. On the one hand I was still regularly attending church, playing the organ and being in the forefront of all the activities. On the other I was enjoying a wonderfully exciting and fulfilling life of spiritual searching and discovery which took me far outside the dogma of our church.

Some time later I was lent a book which discussed a number of types of mediumship. This included the subject of automatic writing. The theory suggested that by sitting in a relaxed manner, with pencil lightly held over paper, someone from the other side would move the pencil and communicate. This, for some reason, appealed to me. I followed the instructions. To my utter amazement the pencil began to move. With what I felt had to be beginner's luck, I began to practise my automatic writing on a regular basis, trying to fit it in at the same time each day when I could. I took the task seriously, starting with meditation and then praying for protection. I had a cross sitting on the desk and a lit candle. Soon words and sentences formed. These were followed by an hour of flowing, smooth, large writing which was unlike my quick scrawl. I believed that the material which came through had strong spiritual overtones. The information included things about the family, friends, the state of the world, advice on personal matters and so on. I began to see myself moving into a life of giving 'readings', handing out helpful advice to those in need. My fantasies and hopes extended to the possibility of getting tips for the stock market so that I would be able to give the entire proceeds to what I considered to be worthwhile charities.

But my ego was not going to be allowed to go wild for much longer. The messages started deteriorating. Dire predictions now came through, together with negative comments about friends and equally disturbing statements about their real feelings for me. I was asked to contact bereaved families with messages from their loved ones - but the names and addresses given did not exist.

The final straw came when I was told my mother was desperately ill. I was told to go to her immediately. With my heart in my mouth, I fortunately thought to ring first. She happily told me she was just leaving to have lunch with a friend. I decided to curtail the development of my questionable mediumistic abilities and resolved never to dabble in such activities again.

I subsequently read a book from the A.R.E. in which warnings were given about the dangers of automatic writing. In the book, automatic writing was placed in a similar category to that of the Ouija Board. My worst fears were confirmed. I realised I was not a clear or - more importantly - a worthy channel. From then on the mere mention of automatic writing brought me feelings of embarrassment and unease. Whenever I felt it was appropriate I told people about my negative experiences in the hope that they would take it as a warning. (I know now, of course, that much wonderful material also comes through from the other side).

My prayers for Mark to have someone special come into his life did not seem to have made any difference. I decided to pray for someone to come into my life so that I might be able to experience a bit of warmth and joy. I was very explicit in my request; it had to be someone in a similar situation, with similar needs, but no one must be hurt, and there must be no children. After about eighteen months of never giving up hope, a fine man did indeed come into my life with all my requirements. A relationship developed and continued for some years. While I hated the deceit and guilt, I loved the romance, the laughter, the support, the communication, appreciation and love for me as a person and, even more, the joy of being able to give in return.

Then one day the man I loved became free of his marriage and suddenly moved away without warning. I had always told him that there was no way I could or would leave my children. I would have understood if he had told me he had found someone else who *was* free, but he gave me no explanation. The experience of deep grief and abandonment, and being unable to tell anyone was agonising. Once again, I felt alone and despairing.

To intensify my sorrow, my loving and supportive mother died not long after. She and I had never discussed my marriage, until one evening, when Mark was working late, yet again, my mother said suddenly, 'I hope you are not staying with Mark because of me. I would understand if you left - in fact I do not understand how you can stay.' Coming from my mother, a pillar of our church which held rigidly to the sanctity and inviolability of marriage, this sudden outburst came as a shock. It became obvious that she blamed herself for my unhappiness in the marriage. I was able to explain that even though she may have felt partly to blame that David and I had not married, my decision to marry Mark was my own, and for that only I was responsible.

After my mother's death, I felt that my last link with the church was broken. I realised that I no longer had to continue my regular attendances, feeling such a hypocrite. Mark had stopped going to church after my father died fairly early in our marriage. As Mark said, he had never believed a word of all that rubbish, but had gone along with it 'just to get you'. This was obviously not an honest thing to have done; but how honest was I, I reasoned at the time, continuing my church attendance with little acceptance or approval of what was taught? In addition, I was committing the unpardonable sin of being unfaithful to my husband.

Once the children had grown up and had left home, a close friend and I started a small business together. This brought me a lot of satisfaction and enjoyment, even though the profits were minimal. At last I had some money which I could call my own. What was more, it was earned by my efforts and I was able to spend it any way I wanted. I was happier than I had been for some years; but even this happiness was to be short-lived.

Mark decided to take early retirement. He wanted to move right away from the city. Suddenly, the life I had built up for myself to help me survive was demolished. In my usual optimistic fashion I decided to make the best of it. Certainly, planning and building a new home was exciting and rewarding. I began to hope once again that a miracle would happen. Perhaps we could now enjoy our retirement together. But history repeated itself once again. I talked about my plans excitedly and took Mark's silence as confirmation.

My expectations included going on short trips by car or even long trips; visiting places we had never been together; quietly entertaining friends (unlike the large impersonal business dinners and parties we used to have in our home, which I had enjoyed, but I felt that now we could enjoy closer friendships). There would be a new garden to create - this time together. There was every chance that our lives would be different. The changes I hoped for did not eventuate. We remained two people sharing a home without any other communication than the necessary mundane matters. We rarely ate our meals together, although this was not new. It had begun when the children were small. At that time, I felt Mark did not wish to be involved with the feeding and getting to bed of small, tired children. But even as they grew older, meals were served at two different sittings - the first for the children and me, and the second for Mark. When not travelling, he usually arrived home later than the mealtime. If he arrived before I served the meal, it became habitual for me to ask if he wanted his dinner yet - and the seemingly automatic reply was, 'Not yet. I'll have it later.'

The exceptions were birthdays and Christmases. These were always special meals, and the cloth my mother had crocheted for me for my twenty-first birthday was used, as was the good Wedgewood china and embossed silver cutlery. Somehow it had become a tradition to serve pink and white marshmallows in one crystal bowl and Cadbury's milk chocolate pieces in another. The birthday gifts were placed on the chair of the birthday person. Mark usually came home in time for the children's birthdays, but on one occasion he did not arrive for his own special dinner. We waited for over an hour and finally ate our share of the goodies. The children went to bed and I worked at my sewing. I wondered how Mark felt when he walked in and saw the table still with its festive decorations, a few remaining marshmallows and chocolate squares, and his birthday cake still resplendent on its silver stand. He opened his gifts and went to bed, and gave no explanation. I asked for none and made no comment, assuming that he preferred to celebrate his birthday with his mates from work than with me and the children.

Incredibly, on one occasion Mark did not arrive in time for our Christmas dinner and gift giving. His family and mine always spent Christmas Day together, and this particular year, because a family member had another commitment on Christmas Day, it was decided to hold our festivities on Christmas Eve. There was always a party at Mark's work, but that was held during the afternoon and was finished before evening. I had obviously not asked him if it would be convenient, but had just announced that I would have the dinner ready by 6.30 p.m., so it would not get too late for the children who were still quite young. We finally had dinner an hour later than planned and still there was no sign of Mark. The gifts were given out and finally the children were put to bed. Just as the 'oldies' were about to leave, Mark arrived. Whatever he had been doing was obviously preferable to Christmas Eve with the family. No one ever again suggested holding the family Christmas at any time other than Christmas Day.

Mark chain-smoked, drank heavily, overate and during his working life, held a high-stress position. I had feared for many years that he was becoming a prime candidate for a stroke and that I would have to be the one to care for him if this happened. I thought that in a good marriage the happiness that had been shared would sustain one in such a situation. But, dear God, how would I cope, with no shared anything to make it bearable and with the additional burden of so many of the deep resentments that I now held.

Unknown to me, twelve months previously, Mark's doctor had given him a referral to see a specialist. Mark finally made the appointment eight weeks after we moved to our new home. We were told he had a massive malignancy between his tongue and his jaw and that surgery was imperative to allow for even a thirty per cent chance of recovery. The surgery involved the removal of his lower jaw and his tongue. They would save a bit of tongue, if possible, so he could perhaps learn to speak again.

Can you imagine the horror of it - all suggested calmly and unemotionally as if it were an ingrown toenail to be removed? The good news apparently was that some months after the surgery a shoulder blade could be removed and used to build a new jaw, and of course plastic surgery would need to be done.

For once Mark actually asked me what I thought he should do. I felt he had more chance of survival without surgery, which promised to be horrendous and mutilating. I told him that I believed he should, before anything else, have spiritual healing from a friend, Marion, who had a meditation and healing clinic. Mark did not appear to be overly enthusiastic at my suggestion, but he agreed to go, saying 'Well you know I don't believe in any of that stuff, but I will go for your sake Annie - as long as there's no mumbo jumbo'. I reassured him on that point, and he did refuse surgery, preferring, as he said, some quality of life. He attended Marion's clinic each time he had to go to the hospital for treatment. Mark suffered no hair loss or side effects from chemotherapy, but after the radium treatments were completed he was told that the tumour, though reduced in size, was still there. Nothing more could be done except by surgery. Meanwhile, the spiritual healing continued. Some months after Mark's medical treatments ceased, the doctors told him that the tumour had gone.

We read in a book about drugs and treatments for cancer that quite often, when a tumour is radiated through a bone, the bone can eventually become affected. Many trouble-free years later, a spot did appear in the jaw bone at the place where the radiation had been directed. This may or may not have been the reason for Mark's subsequent illness. The cancer had returned, and this time there was no medical treatment Mark could have, except the radical surgery initially proposed when the cancer was diagnosed eight years before. Again he refused to have the surgery. When weakness ultimately prevented the long trip to Marion's clinic, he received absent healing from her. Over the many months of ensuing physical deterioration, Mark remained comparatively pain free and required a relatively small amount of morphine. His final illness was prolonged well beyond the expectations of the doctor who commented on his physical strength. We all believed this was due entirely to Marion's help. It was an extremely difficult time, but my admiration for Mark's courage and desire to keep going, no matter what, knew no bounds. He was determined not to go to hospital or to have any outside help. Mark had always been the Big Boss. Never once did he relinquish the role.

As Mark's condition worsened, he became even more angry. This is what I found the most difficult aspect of his illness to cope with. On one occasion after an obvious show of frustration and anger with my inability to understand what he was trying to communicate, he wrote a note saying 'I am not angry with you, but at THIS' - pointing to his poor face.

During the long months, I thought often of the irony of this situation. For so long Mark had been reluctant to communicate with me in any way. Now when he perhaps would have liked to have done so, he was unable because of his physical condition.

I had been house-bound for many months, with my nursing responsibilities almost totally consuming my waking hours. The doctor suggested to Mark that he go to a hospice for a short time 'to make him more comfortable', but in reality it was to enable me to have a short break. Mark agreed to go for one week only. The doctor told me to rest and not to visit for a few days. Mark was told I was not well enough to visit him.

It Is Never Too Late - Chapter 1

The day before Mark was to return home his condition suddenly worsened. As soon as I could I went to him. I walked into his room with my usual greeting. Mark opened his eyes, leaned forward and grabbed each of my hands with great intensity. The tears began to run down his face as he kept holding me and saying 'Oh, Oh, Oh'. He could not speak, but I saw the love in his eyes and felt it pouring through his hands into mine. I suddenly knew he loved me but probably had not realised it himself - and the love I felt from him overwhelmed me. All the anger and resentment fell away in an instant. For half an hour I stood beside him with his grip never lessening; suddenly I had 'permission' to hold his hand and to stroke his head - something I could never have done in all those years.

The miracle was that we had five more days together. He drifted in and out of his body, and then one evening he did not come back.

The Writing

In spite of my resolve never to try automatic writing again, I felt my right hand begin to tingle on two occasions. The first time was only a few weeks after my mother died. I took up my pen and rested it lightly on a blank sheet of paper. The following was written: *'Anne, we wish to write. Aforementioned writing has only wasted our time. Writing for self is worthless. Many of us only want to help. Anne, here is your wonderful mother'*. Very slow and laboured writing followed. I knew it was my mother from the pet name she called me. She thanked me for all I had done for her while she was in hospital. She went on to say what a lovely happy time we had when I visited her with all the children. We had sat around the bed eating pizzas and chatting about everything and anything in the way she had always enjoyed. She appeared to be unconscious, but I had felt she was totally aware of what was going on and enjoyed hearing it all. *'When I passed through the tunnel, Dad and Stephen were there and my Mum and her Mum's...'* The writing had just stopped in a wavy line as if there was no energy left. That was it.

At the time I did not know who Stephen was, but I later realised it was the first name of an old minister who often visited us when I was a child. He had taught my mother to play the church organ.

I told no one. The second time occurred as I worked at my desk. I felt the now familiar sensation in my hand and I put pen to paper in the required way. This time the communication was supposedly from an uncle whose death notice I had seen a few weeks previously. We had lost touch because he and his family were not members of our church.

'Anne, please tell my daughter...', and the communication went on to thank her for specific things she had done for his comfort and help. He expressed his regret that he had not been able to thank her adequately. He said he was now free from pain, free to move, and able to see clearly. I did not feel that his

daughter would be receptive to the way in which I had received the message.

Instead, I wrote to her expressing my sympathy at her bereavement, and then added that I had had a clear dream in which her father had looked so young and well and in which he had asked me to tell her - and so on. I did not expect any acknowledgment, but many months later I met her unexpectedly. I casually asked if she had received my letter, and if it had made sense. Happily for me she said it had. When she explained the nature of his illness and how she had helped him, his words made complete sense to me as well.

Many years passed during which I had no other experiences of this nature. Then, only two weeks after Mark's death, I felt a strong energy in my hand which again I could not ignore. What followed was a gift beyond imagining, a gift that opened for me a whole new way of thinking and believing.

Chapter II

The Communications Begin

I was at my desk, when I suddenly felt the familiar tingling in my hand. Somehow I just knew it was Mark, though logically it did not make sense. This time, I began writing: "Mark, you know I do not wish you back. I just wish we could have communicated more, and that you knew that I cared. I wish I could have told you and known that you understood and accepted my love with total belief. I was so proud of you." Then the slow writing began:

(Mark): "Annie, Annie, Annie, - more ways of communicating than words. I knew you greatly cared and wanted the finest for me. You always made the best of every situation. Now you must go on without regrets, as going back is pointless. I made many mistakes and I am so sorry. Please keep in touch. For a while I am resting, but I feel great, and I am proud of *you*." Two days later I took up my pen again, but this time the writing began with no opening question or comment from me.

(Mark): "Annie, please give me a little time. It is all so strange. Mother - mine - was here, and Dad. My first feeling was most peculiar, and then I was not in the nurse's room, but up on the ceiling. Then I saw Mum and Dad, so young and strong. Mum took me by the hand, and said my great worries were over and I was safe. Dad just smiled. He has all his teeth[1] and so

---

[1] Mark's father had a dread of dentists, and as he grew older refused to have any dental work done. He had four front teeth missing for a number of years, but managed to hide the gap by pulling his top lip down, and smiling very carefully.

do I, and my face is perfect and so is my body. I wish you could see me. Later on, after you had made the trip in to see me, more people came, mostly relatives, and looking young. We walked and it was wonderful to speak clearly again. All of the relatives were there and they opened my eyes to the beauty around; flowers, trees and music and such colours, more than I have ever seen. As we walked and talked I felt weak and I was taken to rest. I will meet lots more of my friends soon. Annie, I always listened to your thoughts about the after life, so I was not really surprised. I wish I had given more attention to you, Annie. I was very difficult and you were so patient. I did not do much for you and now I realise it."

(A): "Was it difficult when you died?"

(M): "No difficulty at all. One minute I was in hospital, and the next I was feeling great. Mum and Dad were here when I came over, but they were only there for a while. They were both so young."

(A): "It must be all so exciting and marvellous."

(M): "Much more marvellous when you find your Annie thinks you are not so bad after all."

Understandably, that comment made me feel quite emotional. I asked whether he remembered being there before.

(M): "Of course. It is coming home. I was not sick at all. I was very well and so full of life - if I can say that. Many are ill, many are tired, but not me. I had all that marvellous help from receiving the healing."

I was always called Anne and I preferred not to be

called 'Annie'. One day I met a friend who insisted on calling me Annie. I tactfully reminded her of my preference, to which she replied, "Oh? I think Annie suits you better." It would of course have been wiser not to have told Mark because from that time on he too called me Annie. I particularly disliked it when he used it on official social occasions.

When Mark first wrote, he repeated the name Annie a number of times. It seemed as though he was identifying himself. As we continued to communicate, the name came to mean something very special to me; it was like an endearment.

(M): "The first time I had so much help, but I was really very well. What I did not say was that in the last few months of my illness I was already spending time over here. When you saw me 'out of it' during the day, I was out of my body. So it was good you did not try to rouse me. I would not have thanked you. When I came back into my body I simply felt I had been asleep and could not remember where I had been. During those last months I never felt a fear of dying. I just knew it would be all right. I found peace and acceptance, but I still wanted to be *boss*. Up to a point, I was in charge even in hospital[2]. They allowed me to feel that, and it was such a comfort. You can regain your whole self image when there is thoughtfulness and loving care. There is so much cruelty for the very

---

[2] Mark was in a wonderful hospice for the two weeks prior to his death. The family and I also received much support and comfort there. Staff counsellors kept up a continuing contact with me for many months after his death.

ill. It is as if they have ceased to exist or have no feelings at all.

To go back: I heard Sister say, 'That is the last of the bottle Mark[3].' Then I felt quite strange and there I was up on the ceiling looking down at some poor creature with its face nearly covered with bandages, and with tubes and bags and things. Then the Sister felt its pulse and rushed out.

It was then that I saw Mum and Dad beside me, both absolutely beaming, and looking so young; and as I told you, Dad had all his teeth. That is what I found most amazing. Mum said, 'Well Mark, your suffering and troubles are over', and then we were in another place: such beautiful trees, flowers and colours like I had never seen and could never describe. Then the relatives came, all young and happy, and then I was taken to rest."

We continued a two-way communication - questions from me, answers from Mark, with added comments and explanations from each of us. We usually wrote once a week for about an hour, which seemed to be the amount of time for which Mark could hold the necessary energy.

The writing did not always go smoothly. Occasionally it was laboured and hesitant, and the meaning unclear. Mark explained that when I was weary, concerned or upset it was like working through a dark

---

[3] Mark had always been a 'Scotch' man, and was still given his evening drink mixed with ice - he insisted on the ice - even though it had to be given through a tube. What incredible love and understanding those nurses showed.

mist, which made the writing much more difficult to do. He said the process is very complex, and I was not an experienced channel. However, as I became more experienced, I began to sense when the channel was unclear, and I would then leave the writing for another time.

Mark wrote of what he called the self-judgment. He said he was shown the events of importance in his life from a spiritual or soul level and they were not those perceived as important by earthly values. "Growing here is not easy, but I am more remorseful, more aware."

In spite of the comfort most of the writing brought to me, the lurking unease of doubt remained with me. What if this was not Mark but a wish fulfillment being projected from my subconscious? Even worse, what if there were mischievous entities having great fun at my expense?

Eventually I asked for proof. I asked if I could be told something I did not know, something that could be checked. Mark directed me to go to a particular drawer in his bedside table where he told me I would find a bunch of keys. 'One of them belongs to the front sliding door.' I was sure that we had only one key to that door and it was hanging in the laundry, but I followed his instructions. To my joy, one of the keys did fit. Back at my desk, the words came, 'Now do you believe?', followed by an even larger 'GOOD!'

In spite of this, I still had periods of self-doubt and an on-going fear of failure, as I remembered my first experience with automatic writing all those years ago. I had still told no one. I believed that my close friends would be aghast at my being involved again in what they would have seen as an egotistical venture, even though they shared many of my beliefs. I naturally wanted this attempt to be genuine, but I wanted to maintain the option to discontinue, if it did not prove to be so. Mark suggested that I type out the first two communications about his death experience, the help he had received, and any other information I had wondered about, and send it to Marion. He thought that her great gift of spiritual understanding and insight would enable her to judge whether the communications were genuine.

With some apprehension I sent off a number of pages. Marion phoned me immediately, and put my fears to rest, and confirmed many of the things that Mark had said. I was at last able to accept that it was indeed Mark who was communicating.

(M): "So much of our life was a tragedy, but it was a karmic situation and now it is over. You were so lonely most of your life, and now that you are really on your own, you are not so lonely."

I certainly did not feel lonely. I knew with certainty that Mark was now aware of how the children and I had felt. He often asked for my forgiveness for different situations that had occurred. He also told me repeatedly how helpful it was that I had forgiven him, and how it was helping him to progress. This meant that my forgiveness was mutually beneficial. He explained how painful it is for people on the other side to be aware of anger, bitter memories and non-forgiveness by those they left behind. He added that this awareness comes without exception to those whose actions caused the feelings.

On the other hand, I knew he now understood the person I had been during our marriage and why I had acted as I did. He forgave me too. The one thing I could not bring myself to mention was the affair I had had. I knew that he must know. He once said that he blamed himself for driving me away and I wondered if that was what he had been talking about.

About six months after our weekly chats began, my fears of failure surfaced once again. Mark wrote of experiences he had had, of which I had no knowledge. I could not accept the information conveyed as it did not correspond with what I thought I knew. I felt it was not Mark but some other source taking over. I was very upset - not so much at the subject matter, but rather that the writing was not from Mark.

During the following weeks I tried briefly to write again but stopped when the same information was repeated. After much thought and prayer I realised that the actual words could indeed be from Mark, and why not? I tried again. Mark began by apologising for not making sure that I was ready to hear a further confession, and then added:

(M): "I thought you would be pleased to hear I was constantly unfaithful to you, as you could then stop feeling so guilty over your love affair."

It Is Never Too Late - Chapter 2

There are no words to express the shock I felt at reading those words. Mark, who used to speak with such disapproval of those 'womanisers', as he called the men who were flagrantly unfaithful to their wives, was finally confessing to having been one of them.

(M): "I put on a good show as far as morality was concerned. I could be quite charming, you know, and full of good humour. I just never showed those qualities to my wife and family. I cannot explain it. When my job took me away from home, I had the opportunities and I took them."

Although I was shocked, I began to experience a feeling of great freedom. We talked over the irony of it all and I told him of my prayers that he would meet someone to fill the void in our unsatisfactory relationship. As Mark said, 'Little did you realise - ha! ' (Mark had begun to put 'Ha!' after some of his tongue-in-cheek comments, and I often laughed heartily over his dry remarks followed by a 'ha!'). Many episodes in our life that I had found bewildering were gradually clarified. I came to an even greater peace. We were able to freely discuss a myriad of situations with total acceptance, forgiveness and understanding. A year after he died, Mark began, "Annie, now we are alone without each other, but we are closer than we ever were." It was true of course. One day I thought, 'If only I had realised what you were really like - the wonderful, loving, caring person with whom I can communicate so honestly, with whom I can laugh, who knows me so well but loves me in spite of it.'

(M): "I was never the man you now know. The person I portrayed was quite different. Just remember how it was and look forward - no regrets."

Mark had tuned into one of my concerns and reassured me: "You have no secrets from us here, but you have privacy. I can tune into feelings and emotions, but no one is watched and listened to at all times".

(A): "Have you had any breakthroughs this week?"

(M): "My big breakthrough was to learn that we made a reasonable success of our marriage. That is because, even though it was a karmic situation of great difficulty, we saw it completed. We also gained strengths. You, because you had to cope alone, and the strength I gained was more to do with all the difficulties of my illness. That was my finest hour or period. Certainly the last years were not your easiest, but, because of the lack you felt, you began to search and study and turned to the spiritual, finally even being able to leave the church without guilt or anger. From here, success is not measured by happiness, but by love and service given, responsibility taken and lessons learnt.

Marriage as it was known is almost a thing of the past. Women are getting their power back; but power has to be shared - not more for one or the other in a relationship, but shared.

You are wondering what I now consider important in a marriage. The important things are love, a willingness to listen, good humour and, most of all, consideration of the partner's feelings in every facet of the partnership. So many broken marriages now have not been given a fair trial. Time to work at a marriage is very necessary. Well, we certainly had that, but I never worked at ours. It existed and that was it." I asked what our lessons were this time. Mark answered:

"Our lessons were to make the best of a very difficult situation, which we did - and most of the ways we found are not what I would recommend."

I asked what we should ideally have done.

(M): "Been able to honestly discuss it all, accept it as most unsuitable in many ways - and divorce; but that was not an option. It was a karmic situation and one we needed to experience. You wanted love and companionship. I did not want closeness. I wanted a physical relationship, a housekeeper, and children as a mark of my virility."

Honesty like that brings a whole new way of evaluating and understanding a relationship. We were able to discuss so many personal situations without rancour or emotion on my part. Mark said simply: 'Forgiveness is not forgetting. It is remembering without bitterness.'

That summed it all up perfectly. Many copies of the writing were filed away in the two and a half years of communication. I was still embarrassed, to a point. I always destroyed the original. I did not want to risk the chance discovery by the family or visitors of the strange-looking writing. In addition to our personal discussions, Mark wrote many things about his new life and experiences, his observations and the lessons to be studied. One day after I had spent some time discussing my activities, I asked about his.

(M): "All of my time is spent in making preparations for more messages to you, Annie - only kidding. I am learning to control my thoughts, which is a great step forward. I go to places and can stay awhile. You will find it much easier here, because you meditate and can still your mind."

Mark had written on such a variety of subjects. I hugged it all to myself with secret delight. I finally confided in two friends. I told them about the writing and shared some of the information I had received. Their interest and enthusiasm about it made me wonder seriously why this wonderful thing had happened. I knew it was not due to any special quality of mine. I thought of the peace of acceptance and forgiveness Mark and I were both experiencing, and the knowledge I had received about his new life. Was this given to me only for my personal satisfaction, knowledge and comfort?

I began to think of the possibility of compiling Mark's words into a book. My friends continued to encourage me until eventually I made the commitment to write about our communications. I could see how wonderful it would be if my experiences could be used to give others a sense of hope. I now knew without doubt that death does not have to have such a sense of finality; on the contrary, it can be seen as a new beginning for us all.

It Is Never Too Late - Chapter 2

The communications changed again. Mark wrote even more fluently and easily and I was astounded. He suggested I go over his previous writing and pick out the subjects I wanted clarified and enlarged. He would then do his best to write about them in more detail, where appropriate.

(M): "The big message is that life goes on, and that on Earth you are *never* alone. Your guide is always there with you and your guardian angel is on call. Your loved ones here still love and care for you and *know* of all the hurt and disappointment they caused.

What you are doing is to help others who carry unfinished business, to realise it is never too late to forgive. Everyone's experience in the now is the most important part, but it is of interest to see the after life through the eyes of someone like the person I was, or portrayed.

When I first came over, I was actually growing in another direction. I wanted to help with the trees, then with the poor starving people. Then I had to make a choice. I could either grow by helping you, or by doing my own thing. As I have told you, there is free will here, but you can see the results of your choices more clearly. So it was made very clear the difference it would make if I wrote with you, especially given our life and experience together.

So I changed my course, as it were. You had to get confident that the writing was genuine, and learn how to do it. My writing and communication had to improve. So there you have it. Naturally it has not only been me.

I have had so much help, as this is a very important assignment. Anything that can take away the fear of death, or help people realise the value of wanting to understand and forgive each other is so important.

Our marriage makes both the book and our communication so much more valid than if we had been an average happy couple. Your big thing, Annie, has been your forgiving nature, and, in a way, your feelings of inadequacy have helped. You thought it was your fault, so you did not altogether blame me for the way I treated you. You do not hold terrible thoughts of pay-back which is a very difficult karmic burden.

I would like to speak about the reason you need to write this book. There are many books written by so-called channellers. Some are excellent and some are channelled by mischievous, ego-centred entities who are writing a lot of stuff that is far from reality. So many people are genuinely seeking, but they realise the falseness of some of the teachings which are available.

You are not a learned academic with a vocabulary to match, and neither are you a way-out New Age extremist. You are a middle-of-the-road thinker. You have an unshakeable faith in the goodness of God, and your belief is in a Cosmic God rather than a God of the select few. You have prayed for help to write a book to take away the fear of death. Your prayers were heard, and now it is time to put it all together."

I expressed doubt about my ability to write well enough to make the book acceptable and readable or of a quality worthy enough for the subject matter.

(M): "More ropes are made with growing vines than with silk. In other words, simple writing will be more widely read than very lofty writing (as you put it). It all has its place, but anyone could read yours and understand it. Mind you, they may not approve of it or believe it - but they would find it readable.

The only way you can write a book like this is to have first-hand knowledge. Mediums have it, but usually in a more general sense. Forgiveness is so important, and strangely it is not often mentioned. Maybe it is because people do not feel it is as important as I now do. While love is spoken of constantly, forgiveness is much neglected.

You are wondering when I was told about your book. I knew you were thinking of writing a book to do with your beliefs, but you did not know whether to write it in the form of a novel or as an account of how your faith and belief had evolved from when you were a child, to your inner knowing now of what truth is to you. The form it has taken was not told to me until you had made the decision to write. I was very surprised and a bit apprehensive about my ability. As you know, communication was never a strong point! But my Teachers said it would be fine. When you listed all the subjects we had discussed, I realised I now had much more to offer. Your prayers have gone up for a long time. Really, even though you yourself did not know the exact form it would take, you have always had a deep desire to share your knowledge of the after life.

You are also wondering whether anyone else here knows about your book and when they knew. It has not only been known, but it was *planned* here and you were *impressed* or *guided*, but being impressed is stronger than being guided."

From this point on I began to organise myself better and included regular working hours with Mark whenever it was possible. I always started with prayers and meditation. Fast, fluent writing followed for up to two hours and it was clear and neat, in contrast to my own untidy scrawl. The writing that came through now was quite different from the original writing, which had been much larger, with all the words joined together, and because of this the deciphering and copying had taken more time. Now, these legible, separated words were a joy to work with. Mark sometimes asked whether I would like a break, but added that the energy was excellent if I wished to continue. He had earlier explained that once I had made the commitment to write about our experiences and communications, he had received much more help from teachers and other helpers. They not only helped with the content of the writing, but also provided the extra energy needed to enable him to communicate for longer periods of time.

On occasions, after we had finished, I would think of something else I wanted to know and would ask for a further comment. But my hand would remain perfectly still, no matter how much I wanted the answer or comment. This delighted me as I saw it as further confirmation that my hand was being used for a purpose. It was not my will that caused the writing, even though I could stop it any time I chose.

My goal was to type out everything that I had received on the day that I received it. I was constantly amazed at what had come through my hand. It was never implied that I should change my lifestyle so that I could give more time to 'The Book'. I soon realised that I was re-evaluating my priorities and I found myself wanting to give less time to some things than I had before.

One morning a phone call from a friend interrupted our work. I mentioned to my friend how much I needed to do before Christmas: mailing cards, wrapping gifts, and the usual baking and cleaning. When I returned to the writing, Mark said: 'Annie, I had not realised how much you want to do before Christmas. Leave the writing now. The book can wait - Christmas will not.'

This was one example of many little asides and comments and suggestions for my well-being that reinforced my feeling of being utterly cared for.

Our communications continued. Mark wrote about many aspects of his new life, his experiences and the knowledge he was gaining. I was constantly amazed at the insights he shared with me. But, as he reiterated, they are an account of his experiences, his perceptions, his ideas, which, though shared by many, are not necessarily shared by all.

Early Experiences And Learning

I had done a wealth of reading and was familiar with various accounts of the life after death. Mark's experiences confirmed much of what I had read. The writing became increasingly more fluent. Mark's knowledge of different subjects continued to expand; but I still had not mastered the technique of detachment. At times I would actually stop writing when I thought that there could be a better word than the one offered. I would search in the thesaurus or check in the dictionary for an exact meaning, or to find a word I considered more appropriate. I am amazed, in retrospect, at how presumptuous I was. I eventually realised that my over-enthusiasm must be inhibiting the communication. I apologised profusely and promised to keep my mental interruptions out of the way and to allow the writing to flow on its own.

(M): "Well Annie, you are letting me write without interruptions or arguments or going to the thesaurus to find a word. Ha! I will believe it when I see it.

Today I will write about the day-to-day experiences and lessons from the beginning - as it was for me. Much of what I will say is mentioned in books on the after-life and channeling, but this is about *my* experience and what I have learned.

When you first arrive it is all so simple - lots of beautiful colours, flowers and beauty. Just as love is a feeling you cannot describe, so it is with what you experience here. It is such a joy to see members of your family who have died and know they love and accept you, and to see them all so young and well, and perfect really. It is as if you see the beauty of their inner beings - not just the outside features. So *everyone* has beauty. That is difficult to imagine, I know, but that is how it is. Gradually you begin to realise you are not just going to float around for eternity looking beautiful and happy. It is then the lessons begin.

On Earth the lessons are often of the spirit. By that I mean you need to learn spiritual values. Here you need to learn how to use the mind. It is very much mind power and mind control - no dense body to keep you grounded, as it were, but a mind that moves your etheric body wherever it likes. What you think is what you get, to coin a phrase. The main thing I had to learn was to handle my new 'air body' as I felt it to be. At first it was so light and unmanageable; just a brief thought and it would respond. You need to learn to control your thoughts, which is not easy, especially for me. I always had such determination to do what I wanted and there I was, not able to move or not move as I wished. Even worse, I had people telling me what to do and giving me no way out of it. There was nowhere to go and no one to appeal to except the ones who were there to help me.

It is essential to learn this mind control for another reason. Your thoughts are seen by all who have learnt the skill. At first you are not able to read others' thoughts; they have to be given to you; but your thoughts, no matter how negative, cannot be hidden. That was one of the most off-putting things I found in the beginning. For someone who kept his thoughts hidden and his face expressionless when it suited, it was very, very difficult to realise I could hide nothing of the inner me, and my thoughts would not have made a pretty picture. Here was a Being of Love and Light suggesting I do something, and I was literally screaming mental abuse in my determination to continue being boss, as I have always been. But then, I am not a fool when it comes to bowing to the inevitable, so I finally began to listen and accept. Besides, you realise the patience and non-judgment of your helpers, and the sooner you accept the inevitability of the situation the sooner you move on. You know how determined I always was to get to the top.

You have to keep your mind absolutely still, in one thought as it were. As you practise meditation, Annie, it will be much easier for you; but stilling the mind to the point of being able to control where you are or whether you move around, with no direction, is even more difficult than meditation. At least with meditation you can let your mind wander and not find yourself somewhere else!

I found it very difficult to keep my thoughts focused sufficiently in one place. In the beginning you are still dense with vibrations from Earth, but as you accept your new situation, you become lighter. You get much help and are not just left on your own; but the time comes when you want to move on and explore, not only here, but on the Earth plane. And that is when the difficulties arise. I had no problem visiting you, but to visit another country and stay and observe is another matter entirely. I would think of where I wanted to be - say an area where the trees are being destroyed - and I would suddenly be there. But if my mind wandered for an instant and I thought, 'If they keep this up it will be like the Sahara,' well, there I would be, over the Sahara. So you have to learn to totally control your thoughts. But you have your guide, who really never leaves you, and teachers are always available. When the necessary control is learnt, it is very exciting to begin to travel. You still do not go on your own, but you can visit all the places you have wanted to see.

Then begins the opportunity to study and learn in Halls of Learning or classrooms. Any subject can be studied thoroughly with the best teachers who know everything up to the present time. There are laboratories for those interested in research. There are places for the musicians, the composers, the artists. You can continue the subject you loved or you may fulfil a dream and do what you were never able to accomplish.

You, Annie, will be able to paint, for instance. You were blocked from that by your parents because of nude models baring their all - ha! But seriously, you would have been a fine artist, I am told. Never mind, there is always here, and there during the next time.

Those who are not studiously inclined spend their time doing what they like best. With their minds and thoughts they can have or build or form whatever they like - a dream home, a country estate, whatever. They can live there and wait for their partner to arrive, and many do. If a brand new car was always a dream, they can have that; but there is not much point as all you need to do is think of travelling and you can. But if a car is what they want, they can have it."

Mark continued: "It is the same with food. You can enjoy the flavour, but it is unnecessary, so gradually you forget about meal times. Drinking and smoking are quite different. To give up on Earth is much easier than to give up here. The addiction or longing remains and there is nothing you can do to get the satisfaction of the addiction - no matter how much you smoke or drink. Smoking and drinking are spoken of so much on Earth, but *in moderation they do not harm the body as much as nasty and negative thoughts and words do.* Drinking and smoking excessively, as I did for so long, does cause great problems which are hard to overcome here. As I said, my illness, which forced me to give up smoking and most of my drinking, made things a lot easier for me here in that regard.

There is the history of the world to be seen - not as known on Earth, but as it really was. Imagine learning the history of the world from the time of its creation, for instance. There is nothing on Earth to cover it. To mention more modern times - what an eye-opener to learn the history of a country as it really was and not just as it was taught by word of mouth or false records, or as written by politically biased historians. It is fascinating, and a mind-bender in some instances. Not all the baddies were bad, and not all the goodies were good.

With all the avenues for recording present world events, things cannot be totally hidden or lost. Even so, the media, which again is made up of individuals, has much to answer for - not only for presenting facts and events wrongly, but for spreading fear, hatred, mistrust and intolerance. How much the media affects you depends on your ability to think and on your own perceptions. When a whole nation is fed untruths and has no way of knowing the way things really are, then of course it is a different matter.

How large would a book need to be to chronicle all the events as the Earth historians know them. Imagine the amount of information available here. You are able to learn all that has ever been, in its truth. And what is truth? When it comes to the future or the present, then truth is not necessarily absolute. Spiritual values remain absolute, but material knowledge on Earth, accepted as true knowledge, is soon obsolete in many instances. Even here, truth changes up to a point, but in the higher realms it becomes absolutely unchanged. At this level, not everything is known, and that is good for you to realise. Many people think that as soon as they pass over they will know everything.

You remember how in some of our earlier sessions you used to ask me about the future - for you, the family, the world - and finally I said that I was not psychic before I died and I am not psychic now. Your thoughts were so strong about what you wanted that it made a thought form. It is like a picture around you and can be seen as an actual happening. So you can understand why so few of my answers came true, much to your concern and adding to your doubts and fears. And so it is with psychics. They are often picking up what you want to happen rather than what *will* happen.

So much is free will - not everything, but many things. Unimportant day to day stuff can be chosen, but big events that concern your whole life are mostly put there for your acceptance, whether you want them or not. That is one thing about being here. Questions such as 'Why did that happen?' or 'Why did I do that?' are clearly answered by the overview of your life. You see the whole picture. It is a marvel of detail and explains so much. You also learn of the experiences and actions in previous lives that dictated what happened in the last one.

Well Annie, you can see it is not like a beautiful day-to-day existence in limbo, doing nothing and waiting for Judgment Day, as some believe. It is a place of learning, understanding, helping where possible, and preparing for the next time around. So far, I am still at the 'helping where possible' stage, and what an incredible experience for both of us. You often shake your head and smile in wonder, as you are now. I cannot say often enough that this is how it was for me. Others have similar experiences, but just as many have totally dissimilar ones.

It Is Never Too Late - Chapter 2

Very strict ideas of heaven bring a very different situation. Many people here group themselves with others of like mind, similar to the way they did on Earth. They have their church, their sermons and their fellowship, and they wait for the Judgment Day when they will then go to heaven and be with God and His angels. Others who believe in sleeping in the grave until the trumpet sounds can literally remain asleep for ages and not awake to the reality of this life. The ones who find it easiest are those with no rigid beliefs either way.

My ideas of further studies had to change when I was given the choice of being with you in a joint endeavour, or doing my own thing as I used to. When it was made clear how important it was for both of us for me to work with you, then there really was no choice. Now we are working together at last, and that is a change from when I was there, is it not, Annie?

To continue: I would have worked in the areas of the deprivation of the planet. It really is in an awful mess. It is hard for you to realise in your beautiful area of fresh air, the ocean and so many trees. But the air is not really fresh, the oceans are polluted, and the planet is so depleted of trees. Urgent help for the planet is needed, with its great problems of lack of food, so much waste and the dire results of increasing toxicity in the earth and atmosphere.

We can help only with our thoughts. It is not like angelic power, which is a force, but rather like giving thoughts to uplift or cheer or even guide if you have reached that stage. I mostly try to encourage, so you see I am finally working on my lack in that area.

You have droughts, floods, fires, man-made destruction and so-called natural disasters. Natural disasters are *all* man-made. Every negative thought of hate, revenge, greed and so on sets up a negative vibration and eventually it gathers into a tremendous force. I am getting off the subject, but in a way it is one of the things I have learned and it is worth passing on. You are thinking of a lecture you heard a long time ago by a Buddhist monk. He said that an action, no matter how seemingly unimportant or slight, can eventually cause a great disturbance or natural disaster; and a member of the audience facetiously said something like, 'Are you telling us that if a butterfly flaps its wings here it will cause a volcano in Hawaii?' Everything has a cause and effect potential - not just potential, but a certainty. So next time you are tempted to explode in anger, think of that explosion building up and destroying a city. It is the same kind of energy. How did we come to discuss this I wonder? My words are rushing along as yours used to - ha!

When our work together is over, I will begin a particular work, if I so desire. At the moment, when not writing with you, I attend lectures and lessons by teachers. No, I do not attend anything to do with business management, but actually I could; new concepts, of course, not ones already known or used. There are many, many subjects; some you would have already studied, but all are new to me.

No great breakthrough in any area of endeavour or research on Earth happens until it is worked out and perfected here. Then someone, or some group that is working on that particular problem or endeavour, is inspired or impressed from here. They may receive it as a sudden flash of an idea, or as a gradual solving of a problem. Even dreams can be used to clarify details of, say, an invention. Most of these occur after very hard study and work and it seems like a natural conclusion to their efforts.

Just think, Annie, you did not just begin to write like this. How much time you have spent and often been so disappointed or discouraged. Finally you found the right purpose, not just for your own personal information, and may I say gratification, but for others. That was when our communication became much better in every way, and that enabled so much more help from here. There are other lessons which are far more personal; about attitudes, past behaviour and whether you can help to right wrongs. I do not mean the self-judgment. That is different again. Sometimes we can help a loved one by constantly bombarding them with thoughts of love or ideas of how to cope materially or just the fact that we are there for them. But if they have a very closed mind, then it is not possible.

The cure for cancer is already known here; but as cancer is so complex and has so many different ways of manifesting, it is not just one simple procedure. Thoughts and emotions play such a tremendous part in both getting the disease and in being cured or having a long remission. Surgery is often unsuccessful because the thoughts that caused the cancer in the first place have not changed, so the cancer or blockage will appear elsewhere.

Aids also, is not a simple thing, and it is *not* because of so-called improper sexual habits. It is to do with not only the immune system of the populace but also the immune system of the planet to which all people are inextricably joined. People are not apart from the planet and all it contains, but are very much held together by the Creative Force or Energy which has so many names, but which we know as God.

I mentioned that on Earth lessons are often of the spirit; that on Earth you need to learn spiritual values. But the lessons are experienced in the physical body. They are so varied, and if learnt they are not repeated. It not learnt they are repeated until they are learnt, either in the same life or in another one. You have seen how women choose a husband or partner who is similar to their father in some respect. Maybe it is a very successful or ambitious man, but one who has no thought for his wife and family; or a drinker, or a wife basher, or both. The lesson is really one of forgiveness. A great dislike of the father's action is permissible, but *not* a great dislike of the father. You are thinking how difficult it is to separate the one from the other and you are right. Lessons are not necessarily easy. As well as forgiveness, it is a matter of realising your own self-worth and not putting up with behaviour that is contrary to your own integrity.

It all sounds so simple and it never is. There are countless aspects as well as the main issues. Some lessons to be learnt on Earth are actually experiences the soul needs and are not to do with karma or past experience or what may be felt to be a failure of some kind. As you know, the soul goes on and on choosing to experience and learn until finally it has experienced fully and can return to God.

The time and complexities involved cannot be readily or fully grasped. I am telling you what I have learned, but I certainly do not comprehend it all yet. Some souls have experienced fully and could be with God, but they agree to return and help the people of the Earth. They are so highly evolved and some are known as holy men and women. Some work in lowly situations and may never be heard of. Some, like Mahatma Ghandi and Mother Theresa, are recognisable as saints. The majority of the exalted ones, however, are never recognised as such and go on with their chosen task in absolute silence or anonymity.

Here you find that the things of Earth that were of paramount importance, such as security, position, power and so on, are as chaff in the wind and hold no weight at all. Love is spoken of and means different things to different people; but 'God is Love' says it all, and it is the love that brings tolerance, understanding, sympathy and all the finer things of life.

When I mentioned the unimportance of prestige and power, I must make it clear that learning and the gaining of knowledge, wealth and power is a necessary part of the physical world. It is how it is used that makes the difference. Any knowledge gained is never wasted, and a refusal to take advantage of opportunities to move ahead in your career, especially when it is for the good of others, is not commendable or even helpful for your own growth.

When I arrived here my mind needed to do a complete about-turn, and for a big boss to be told that he has been on the wrong track all his life, and that he had better get his act together or else...can you imagine! (This is just a bit of humour, because that is never said or even implied. It is all taught so lovingly that you almost feel you are working it out yourself. And when you do get it right, you move on, but not before.)

My learning has been more difficult than any course I ever studied on Earth, but never has any learning been so satisfying and so right. You have always had a feeling for much of what I have learnt and it will be easier for you than it was for me. Of course, you will have other lessons to learn."

Recalling With Regret

"When the time of rest and recuperation is over, and for some it is longer than for others, the time of 'remembering and regrets' begins. This description is more appropriate than the one generally used - Judgment Day, when all will be judged and will go to either heaven or hell. Even if the belief is that this will occur immediately at death, it is still thought of as a judgment from God. It has been so wrongly understood, as the judgment is self-judgment or a total review and overview of our life, by ourselves.

You asked me once if I remembered a particular incident. I said, 'We do not forget anything, unfortunately,' and that is how it is. You hear of people who have almost died, saying their whole life flashed before them. If only it were like that. Not only do we not forget anything, but we are aware of the feelings and emotions of those we have harmed. There are sins of omission as well as commission. Not doing something good can be as harmful as doing something that is not good. Many things we thought were good are not worth anything, and the things we hoped would remain a secret we find were not all that bad - just really not the best thing to do.

This remembering is not done all at once. It is done gradually - the smaller things first and in between are the lessons of coping in a spiritual or etheric body and learning to control the mind. I have explained this more thoroughly elsewhere.

As you are able to face up to your more negative memories, you are helped through them bit by bit. You are never left to do it alone. That would be an impossible task for anyone to perform. There is love and understanding, and *never* judgment, given by your helpers, or teachers, or your guardian angel or guide. You can call them what you like. The frustration is that you cannot do much about any of these negative memories. You need to ask forgiveness for each and every occasion you have harmed someone. Many things for which you felt no regret, you find did in fact have very negative results.

The opposite also applies. The positive parts of your life are shown to you just as clearly - the little acts of kindness or an encouraging word, or generosity in any form at all. An action done deliberately to harm, or as a pay-back, whether emotional, mental or physical, carries a heavy karmic debt. There are no exceptions. This has often to be faced in a future life. Intention has a big part to play as far as the 'recalling with regret' is concerned.

As well as feeling the hurt you caused, if the ones you harmed are still remembering with anger and bitterness, even though you have more or less cleaned the slate of 'review and regret', you are held back by their thoughts and negative memories. Forgiveness on either side is so important and your forgiveness has allowed me to progress to other levels of learning. Here, if you are going through the more negative aspects of your life on Earth and you find the persons involved hold no grudge or resentment, it makes such a difference. If they also forgive and accept your actions as part of the person you were, then what a freeing and wonderful experience it is.

Many of the things recalled are really an awareness of where one has erred. So much of our lives is filled with thoughtless, heedless actions and words, and we are responsible for them. Many parents are blamed for the misdeeds of their children. Up to a point this is correct and parents have to take some responsibility. Your parents and mine would have seen how their actions had a bearing on our future actions and attitudes; but the final responsibility is still ours.

I cannot say too strongly that there is never a time we are left without love, support and understanding. You and I have been blessed beyond description because, after a marriage of non-communication and misunderstandings in every area, here we are, able to remember, discuss and forgive. This can be done by everyone, whether here or on Earth. I do not necessarily mean the actual type of communication we are enjoying. Mental communication is open to everyone - just a one-way communication with no audible answers, just the forgiveness or the asking for forgiveness, and accepting that everyone has their own path and limitations, can be such a healing process. It can all be sorted out and released. This helps the person here to progress, and of course the person left there can get on with their life as well.

Grieving without any understanding or acceptance is so hurtful to both parties. Grief is understandable but is not the proof of love. If some things need to be faced honestly, they need to be accepted as part of the process. If a marriage or relationship has been unhappy, then it is dishonest to pretend that the death is a tragedy or a terrible loss. This is not to say that the person should dance with joy either; but the past needs to be looked at honestly and clearly, and seen for what it was. Then it is time to ask forgiveness, and to do whatever it is that you would like to have done. Release the person from all your more negative memories.

When we had that incredible experience a few days before my death, it was a miracle of forgiveness between us and made this communication so much easier. Considering how separately our lives were lived while we were together, is it not amazing that now we are apart, we are working together so closely?

Perhaps I need to mention other realms. As I have said, here we feel the hurt and pain we thoughtlessly or deliberately inflicted on others; so can you imagine the suffering of those, for instance, who have perpetrated great crimes in time of war, or even so-called peace. There were those who were directly responsible for the degradation, death, torture and so on of the thousands or millions who suffered during the last great war. Not only do they feel the pain and suffering of each individual, but also the grief of those left mourning and destitute. Aeons of ages in your time would be needed to go through those particular judgments. So often you hear it said, 'If only so-and-so knew what I am going through' or 'If only they realised the misery they caused,' or similar remarks. Everyone can be assured that the person knows only too well and feels and regrets it at a deeper level than anyone can imagine."

It Is Never Too Late - Chapter 2

The White Light And Auras

I had often heard of white light. I understood that it was a power from God which could be seen in the spiritual realms. One morning I asked Mark if he would like to write about his perception of it - unless he needed to think about it first.

(M): "Annie, I do not have to think about it, as you have had it in mind for a while, and I have a few comments ready.

The white light was one of the first things I learnt about here, but I could not see it very well. Some see it clearly when they first arrive, but to me it was not obvious. It is very much a part of the spiritual realm and is available to all on Earth to visualise and use; but until people are aware of its existence they do not experience its help. So many go through life, which is really a living death, interested only in material things and not in things of the spirit. By things of the spirit I do not mean religion, but non-material values such as love and compassion, understanding and so on.

When I was alive on Earth I thought of material things as being of *number one* importance in life. Success, power, prestige, privileges and all that they represent were what I saw as the reason for living.

When you pray and ask for the white light to surround a person or a material possession, it appears as if a soft white light has gone on, surrounding the person or area. It always helps and protects, and the more faith you have and the greater the sincerity of your wish or prayer, then the stronger and more powerful the light. In a large group of well-intentioned people, the light can be so powerful that you do not have to ask for it. It is there; and of course the beings of light, or angels as you know them, are all part of it. As you pray, Annie, a white light forms and, depending on what you are praying for, a colour forms as well.

After death some people are unaware of where they are or what they are doing. They can remain in confusion for a long period, but this is where prayer groups on Earth who do rescue work help so much. When they become aware of a lost soul wandering around - and there are many - they tune in to them and explain to them that they are no longer on the Earth plane and that they will be helped to find their way. They are told to look to the Light. Once they do that, they are able to leave the Earth plane and move ahead with the beings of light who are waiting.

Even in the darker realms there are always beings of light, or angels, waiting for souls who want to move from where they are. It has to be the soul's own wish, and until they actually turn to the Light and want the help, they stay where they are. That is where prayers for the dead help so much. Prayers said with sincerity can make all the difference.

You are wondering about Jackie Kennedy's passing and that of well-known people. How they lived and how much service they gave, whether they inspired for good or evil, decides where they are. But when a whole nation mourns and countless prayers are said, as in her case, a huge golden light surrounds the person and their loved ones who are left. It brings strength and helps them to cope with the problems they are experiencing from their loss. Not all notable people have this. Those who have misused their power and privilege have a very rude awakening.

Auras are quite different to the white light. They are a personal thing and, like finger prints, are unique to each person. But unlike finger prints, auras change.

It is not only human beings who have auras, but all living creatures and plant life - rocks, mountains, plains and valleys, countries, cities and even buildings - have their energy field (which sounds more scientific perhaps).

Auras of living things change constantly, but those around people change more than others. It is not just the physical characteristics of a person that determine the aura, but also their thoughts, emotions, attitudes and actions, and these cause the constant changes. Some gifted psychics cannot only see the colours but can also interpret them. The physical colours are the easiest to see as they are stronger; but the spiritual colours are also easy to see, even though they are much softer and often have silver through them. Past lives are also shown in auras, but the colours are very subtle indeed and are not usually seen by the average psychic, and certainly not by me. A physical problem or dis-ease shows in the aura before it manifests in the physical body. It can be seen as a grey spot over the particular area. For instance, a slight problem that could lead to a major illness is apparent long before the symptoms are obvious. An existing problem shows up as a dark grey area, and the energy coming from it is wilting or nonexistent, depending on the seriousness of the situation.

Imagine if doctors had the gift of seeing auras or energy fields and understood their complexity with regard to the physical body. What an aid to diagnosis, and particularly to an early one. Some inventions for more appropriate ways to diagnose illnesses actually show the aura. What untold changes would be made in the health system if these could be used by diagnosticians to correctly interpret the signs, not only of an existing illness, but a probable one. Some day it will be accepted that prevention **is** better than cure. Most people would certainly embrace that adage, but there is much more money, wealth and power in the business of trying to cure ill-health than in preventing it in the first place.

Perhaps here I could mention the effect of negative thoughts. I am sure I do not have to list them, but a few are hatred, resentment, non-forgiveness, fear of the future, and so on. Dwelling on past problems is pointless and is so damaging. It all shows in the aura, which may not seem important, but if the thoughts are continually held, they can then be taken into the physical body and bring about many illnesses and problems. It is not easy to be in a very difficult situation and not feel anger and resentment. It is almost impossible for most people. Being in a physical body you have the limitations of what that entails. If these negative thoughts were recognised for what they are, so much discomfort and illness could be avoided. Being aware of such thoughts, and releasing them to the best of your ability, can be the beginning of a vast improvement in the quality of your life.

Speaking harshly about people and judging them over and over brings what is seen as a wide pattern of discord in your aura. If this continues, the discord goes into our physical body. If only people realised the effects of constantly speaking ill of others. When you catch yourself doing it to excess, the best thing to do is to mentally ask forgiveness of the person and *mean it*. This really helps. When you criticise and speak badly of others, it does not actually harm them - it harms *you*. It is understandable to be angry, to be disappointed, to feel let down and so on, but it is best to try and get over it as quickly as possible and not carry it as a continuing burden. That is when it causes problems to *you*.

It is very interesting to be able to see the energy that comes from different cities and countries. The poor, war-torn countries are very dark; but even there you can see strong light appearing where people still care for each other, where they still have hope, and where they do not succumb to despair, fear and hatred. Countries not at war still have a war against crime, poverty, lethargy and hopelessness. Australia has very dark areas over each city, as do all countries. From on

It Is Never Too Late - Chapter 2

high, as in a space ship, the colours of various countries can be seen - not only the light and dark. It has nothing to do with prosperity or poverty. The country with the whitest light is not one with the highest credit rating and neither is it one with the most magnificent churches. So many things are not as our belief systems have led us to expect. There can be very bright areas around ancient sacred sites and around churches that follow Christ's example; but when churches are judgmental, dogmatic and do not practise 'love thy neighbour', and when they teach the fear of punishment as well, then there is not much light to be seen. Where worship, prayers and meditation are held in all sincerity and love, whether it is in a church, a house, a room or out in the open, there can be seen the white light, as well as soft colours and silver and gold. Nothing is hidden really. So you can imagine the colours, or lack of them, from places of greed, hatred, confinement, cruelty and criminal activities. You should see the strength and softness of the light coming from some non-Christian temples of worship. The amount of light and colour depends on the love and inner beauty of the people praying or worshipping. Without real love and service any church is dead, as is any large organisation where the whole motivation is greed and power and making money.

I mentioned that Australia had dark spots in the cities, but the majority of the country, especially the centre and the west, has a very strong, vibrant energy. These vast areas are still relatively unspoiled by people

It Is Never Too Late - Chapter 2

and retain their original colours. You think the scenic colours you see there are beautiful. They are nothing compared to what we see from here."

As I was writing this I wondered what effect the mining of various minerals would have on the energy or colours of an area.

(M): "Where the mining is done there is a whole new look to the energy. The original energy is cut, as it were; but the company in charge of the operation, and the attitudes of the workers and their reasons for being there form the energy. It is difficult to explain, but greed and manipulation, and wanting to make money for not very worthwhile reasons, brings a very unpleasant energy. This does not mean they should not be mining. Mining is part of the creative plan, and mankind has always used the resources of the Earth; but there are right ways of doing it and ways of bringing much disharmony."

On Prayer

On one occasion as Mark was writing, I suddenly thought I would like to know the most appropriate way to pray.

(M): "As your understanding of the laws of the universe increases, so does your attitude to prayer. What a mess your life could have been if your prayers of what you wanted in the past had been answered to your satisfaction. As you progress, and allow God's will to guide your life, rather than your wants or even your needs, the manner and content of your prayers change.

It is appropriate to pray for certain things, if they are very positive and for the highest good of all. You can pray for peace, for rain, for health for everyone, and for a peaceful passing. You can certainly pray for what you would like to happen in someone's life for their happiness, as you see it. If it is meant to be, it will happen, and if not, it will not. You can pray for specific things for someone else. It needs to be in their best interest, something that is right for them. You could pray for something you think will make their life complete, but it may not. Many pray to have a child, for instance, but they are not really able to cope with their own lives, much less with a child - and maybe it is a karmic situation anyway.

It is quite appropriate to pray for someone or something to help along a situation that is already being worked on. There is no point praying to pass an examination if you have not worked for it, or praying for someone's health if they are not doing anything to help themselves. It is all right to pray for healing and help to add to what is being done already.

The safest prayer, one that will not hinder a situation, is to surround the person or the situation with God's love and light, or the power of the angelic forces. Pray that what is right for the person will manifest. This always helps. That way you are standing back, as it were, and letting God's will be done. Praying for protection is another prayer that always helps. It can be quite specific and is necessary in these times of so much negativity.

Prayers for support and strength, and prayers for forgiveness to others and to self are important. Any prayers help a situation; but prayers for protection are very powerful, whether they are for self, for others or for material things. When injuries and problems still occur, and they do, it can be for a particular lesson, but is not necessarily a punishment. Some people see everything negative as karma. A child can be injured and it is part of the experience of being a child. If a child cuts its finger on glass or a razor blade, it has learnt something - well usually it has. Prayers for the planet and prayers for all on this side are appropriate; we need your prayers as well and are conscious of them being said and the help they give. It comes like light and warmth. Asking for help with things of the spirit will always help, but prayers for worldly wants and needs are not always answered the way you would like. They are always answered, however.

If you pray and your heart is not really in it, it still does not hurt. If you pray it long enough, you will eventually mean it."

Some weeks later, the regular greeting of 'Annie, this is Mark' was not followed by the usual personal comments for me or the family. I thought that what followed would have made a very interesting sermon - it was more helpful than many I have heard!

(M): "I am going to write about what I have perceived, learnt and now know about prayers, and the most helpful way to express them. Prayers are of so many different types - prayers of praise, of supplication for self and others, for forgiveness and so on.

I never really prayed except during the last difficult stages of my illness. Well, I did pray in the beginning for a total remission, which I obtained; but I do not recall that I said 'thank you' very often. My prayers were for not having to go to hospital and to die at home. Once I knew I was not going to get better, I wanted a nice, easy, quick death. I was not afraid, as I have told you. When you spoke of your beliefs, I listened. Even though I did not absolutely believe as you did, I felt it sounded like a logical process, and certainly I had never accepted the heaven or hell idea.

My prayers were always for my comfort. My one and only prayer for anyone else was when you did not come to see me. I wanted so much to see you again. At last I knew what you meant to me, what you had always done, and how I had behaved towards you. It was a necessary revelation. So when you did arrive I was able at last to express my feelings, and even without any words spoken, you understood.

I have been studying the psychology of prayers and their results. Briefly: More people in the East pray than in the West;.more non-Christians than so-called Christians pray; more people pray for members of their families than for themselves; more poor people than rich people pray; more sick people than well people pray. All prayers make contact of some kind, but the most potent prayers are those that ask for protection and those that are prayed in time of need.

You are wondering whether my studies or classes are optional or required. They are mostly optional now, but they were not in the beginning. Your prayers for me help me with my learning. Prayers for me to grow in wisdom would be appreciated.

Some people are constantly worried. Worry achieves *nothing*. Mothers worry about their children. What they need to do is pray for their protection. If they do not pray, it is more beneficial to just let the children do what they need to do and feel that they will be all right. It is not a sign of not caring. It is just that worrying about what may never happen is pointless and if something does happen, what has been achieved? The worry did not prevent it. Concern is quite different. Concern is a feeling of being aware of what is happening and knowing that there is a potentially negative outcome.

I was very interested in how prayers operate. Help comes according to the reason for praying. Ultimately, of course, all help comes from God, but He has His helpers. These range from archangels to a soul making up for misdeeds on Earth. Many family members are helped by their loved ones and their unloved ones - ha! The loved ones do it out of love, and the others, if they want to make amends in some way, can also assist. Of course they all need help to be able to help. The ones who are trying to make amends to their loved ones for their non-caring, or other actions they now deeply regret, are not always able to help very much at first. If their intention is sincere, then there are others more advanced, shall we say, who can help them to help. A matter of urgency can bring amazing, instant aid, just as a warning of danger can be given - and this usually comes from angels.

Can you imagine me even mentioning angels, let alone explaining them? Angels are a spiritual force of energy. Guides and teachers have had physical bodies in most instances, and they help those on Earth by guidance and impression. Free will is almost always allowed to operate, unless it interferes with the person's purpose, or perhaps someone else's pathway.

As you can see, there are no strict or general rules. I can only give you what I see, know and understand at the level I am on now. There are so many planes and realms which I could not explain in my way of expression, even if I knew all about them, which I do not.

Prayer acts like a magnetic field, and people, or should I say beings from here who work in the area of request, surround the person and give their help. Actual healing is done by angelic beings who give power; but help with say a medical problem can be given by those working in the medical field. They can guide the person to a particular doctor, diet, therapy or even a change in lifestyle. The person experiences the help as a sudden idea, or it comes from reading an article, seeing an advertisement, or from a comment the person just happens to hear.

You always said you had a special shopping angel. When you have a particular need and are very focused on exactly what it is, you can find it without looking fruitlessly. When you pray, be absolutely specific with your requests. Affirming, too, is powerful, but prayers are more powerful and get even better results. The names of God in whatever religion you can think of have a power. When these names are used in anger, or even just casually dropped into a sentence without meaning, it causes a drop in your energy. I do not know quite how to explain it. Used in the right way, the names are a power boost. Used negatively, they are a power drain.

Prayers for rain, if said in all sincerity by enough people, bring much power and energy, which can then be transferred by devas who are in charge of the elements. (You are smiling at the thought of me writing about things like that. I am writing what I have learnt, and I also have teachers standing by to help.)

There are some events that only happen in their own good time, and no matter how often you pray, it will not speed up the process. There may be the good of others involved, and it may not be their time. To pray and add 'for the highest good of all' is a way of acknowledging that you do not know what is best, particularly if you are praying for someone else. It is sometimes more appropriate to ask for help for them 'to make the right decision for the highest good of all'.

I remember you talking about how our neighbour could not understand why his wife died after his constant prayers for her recovery. He said that the Bible distinctly says, 'If ye shall ask anything in my name,

It Is Never Too Late - Chapter 2

that will I do' (John 13:14). But as you know, even Jesus prayed, 'Not as I will, but as You will' (Matthew 26:39).

So you can take your pick, depending on how much you think you know what is best. I do not mean that mockingly. It is the way it is. Did Jesus really mean He would give *anything* asked in His name? If Jesus knew everything, as He did, then He would not ask for what was not for the person's highest good. So if you ask in Jesus' name, it is like saying 'I ask as He would ask'. Then you must accept that whatever happens is as it should be. If you ask for what *you* think is best, without a thought of whether it is God's will, then it is as though you are saying that you know what is best, and that that is what God should do. I obviously did not work that out, but maybe it gives you something to think about. It is certainly an explanation to be considered. Any prayer that is just read or memorised, without thought or feeling, is not praying at all. It is just a collection of words. The Lord's Prayer, however, is a very powerful prayer, and even if said thoughtlessly is still powerful. It was given for each individual's needs, and said with conviction helps in every area of your life. The Great Invocation[4] is another prayer of great power. It is said by many people now of different races and creeds. If said enough, the planet could be transformed.

Prayer is so important. Always pray as you speak, naturally, rather than in the stylised form of some <u>churches. It</u> is good to begin with words of praise and

4 See Page 142

thanks. Prayers for forgiveness are often forgotten, and prayers for more purposeful living are not often said. Prayers for loved ones come easily but the troublesome ones in our lives rarely get a mention. Meditation is different, of course, but necessary. One is as important as the other. Pray first and then meditate. Praying is speaking to God, and meditating is listening to Him.

When a person dies, it is helpful and advantageous in every way to have prayers said. The Protestant churches, as a rule, do not agree with this, as their teaching is that, at the moment of death, your fate is sealed, as it were; up or down, depending on your belief or lack of it. (I am not speaking of all Protestant churches, as there are many different teachings about death, resurrection, judgment and so on.) When one of our friends died recently, you wondered about the importance of the Last Rites being said. (By the way, he is fine and resting.) It helps souls to pass over peacefully when that is their belief. I received a different kind of help for my peaceful passing.

You are wondering about the best way to pray for those who have died. When you pray, use your own words. Ask for the angels to help and support the departed one at this time. They are already surrounded with love and light. As time goes on, just think of them with love and, if necessary, forgiveness. And if you have trouble with forgiveness, ask for help for yourself and ask that forgiveness is given to you. That is all you really need to do. A prayer for help for anyone is always heard, even if it is a momentary one. It can be asking for help for the patient when an ambulance flashes by or even when you see someone walking with great difficulty. Hearing of major calamities that seem beyond reach of physical help should always engender prayers. Pray also for your guides, helpers and teachers. Ask for their minds to be open to what *their* teachers are giving to them, and for wisdom and the energy and clarity to then give it to you. When your prayers are answered to your satisfaction, a prayer of thanks is appropriate. A prayer that appears not to have been answered at all may have been even more helpful for your soul's growth, so a 'thank you' still does not go amiss. Prayers of thanks for all your joys and sorrows come under the same heading, as it were, and praise and thanks for everything that is: the creation, the beauty, the daily blessings and being in a physical body to experience and learn and move ever closer to God's eventual plan for us.

This all sounds as if you could just sit and pray all day, but that is not what being in a physical world is all about. It is about love and service and forgiveness while working in a physical body.

You are asking about what happens when two people are praying for opposite results, each believing he or she is absolutely right. Well, it is a case once again of purpose or intentions, and of truth and justice. And also karma plays a part in the lessons to be learnt. It is all so complex and without an overall general rule.

It is necessary not only to ask for what you feel you need, but also to open yourself to what is given. Not always are your prayers answered in the way you would like. Sometimes you need to experience something that is definitely not what you want. I mentioned that I had prayed for a quick, easy death and to not have to go to hospital. The final illness was long, but I found peace and acceptance which I did not have before. The short stay in the hospice was such a blessing for you, Annie, and was really what was necessary for me. The whole experience of my illness was one we both needed to experience to shift our awareness, if I can put it like that. An awareness of there being more to our life together than we had ever considered. So whether you say 'as God wills' or whether you do not, it is all ultimately in His hands.

Prayers For The Departed

Some churches understand the importance of prayers for the 'dead' (as they are wrongly called - they are more alive here than they are there). The way of praying, however, is not always appropriate. The intention of the prayers is often to get the ones who have died out of what is thought to be a very negative situation, which they are not necessarily in at all. You have a prayer for the departed in the talk on Prayer, but I will mention it again. The very best way to pray for them is to ask for the Divine Light to surround them, and to ask for them to receive the love and support of

God and His angels, or helpers, or whatever term suits the belief of the person praying.

All those who come over already have that love and support ready and waiting; but not all are willing and able to accept the help and sometimes have shut themselves off completely by their actions on Earth, and their attitudes, emotions and thoughts which they still retain. Some are really stuck in a very negative situation for a long time and do not move forward at all. There are always beings of light to help, but their presence has to be acknowledged and their help asked for. Prayers can penetrate the darkness and help the lost soul to see the Light and also to see the beings of light."

Chapter III

Masks

Annie, today I am going to write a little about the masks that everyone wears to a lesser or greater extent. A couple can put up a facade of happiness together, but each of them is wearing a mask. You and I certainly excelled at this.

Your mask was that of a happy, easygoing, full of fun, helpful and affectionate person. You were verbal about my shortcomings to a very few close friends, but on the whole, you put on a good face. There you were, unhappy, frustrated, resentful and angry at how our marriage turned out. It did not even go down hill gradually. You were unhappy from the beginning.

You were also wearing the mask of a good Christian, a church-attending woman, taking the children to Sunday School, helping with functions and playing the organ. You were not only taking part in the women's organisations, but were also holding office - with time-consuming responsibilities. You were in the forefront of all the working bees and gave generously of your time and my money - ha! (Just thought I would put that in.) But behind that mask you disagreed with the teachings of the church, and at the same time you judged the attitudes of many of the congregation for their criticism of the minister and their fellow-members. To cap it all you began to be unfaithful to your husband. Oh Annie, how *could* you? That is just a bit of humour, because you found it gave a whole new meaning to your life and you certainly needed it. At least you did not wear a mask for me before we were married, even though you wore one for your parents and the church.

And now for my mask. Before we married I wore a mask of being quite easy to get along with. I listened to your chatter and your ideas of how marriage should be, but I never ever agreed with it. I had my own ideas of what a wife's role was and it was the opposite to yours. The husband earned the money and was boss, and that went for every facet of the marriage; he could do what he liked as long as it did not create too many waves. You were fairly easy to manipulate. You did not really ever fly into a rage. You certainly stated what you would like me to do or not do, but you did not throw a tantrum when I went my own way. So much of the time you were totally bewildered by my actions and my lack of any kind of consideration or co-operation.

Anyway, there I was with my mask firmly in place. At home I wore the mask of being cold, intolerant and a hard-working business executive. I implied that when I was away from home it was nothing but work, work and more work. But with the female office staff I was the genial, sometimes quite humorous man. To the male employees I was hard-working, responsible and totally unwilling to overlook any shortcomings. To my bosses I was ambitious, willing to do anything they required and a man who played as hard as they did; a man whose wife and family need never be considered.

And what was the real me? I do not think I ever questioned it or wondered. But deep down I was unhappy, unsatisfied and lonely, as you intuitively felt and for which you blamed yourself. The thing was, you were unaware of what I was doing to make up for any lack I felt in my home life - a lack for which I was initially totally responsible. Having said that, of course, I was as I was, and the man I portrayed was not who I really am - the person with whom you are now communicating.

This all sounds very personal, but in a general sense I think many people will be able to relate to it. When you compound the individual masks worn by members of a family into a group of masks, how can anyone know what goes on behind the masks and the closed doors, as it were - the doors of the mind as well as the home. It is easy to say 'how could they do that', but perhaps the question should be 'how could they *not* do as they do?', given the true situation of their lives.

Well, that is how I see it now. I remember how intolerant I was of everyone. I was always so sure I was right - at least my masks were. Underneath them I was often unsure and hurt and vulnerable and *not* the big strong man I always showed - or felt I did. Behind what appears to be strength is often weakness, and behind what is taken for weakness lies great strength. But that was certainly not how I understood it then.

Spiritual Healing

When spiritual healing is used (that is, healing without any material source or substance), it can accomplish different types of healing.

There is an actual physical healing or a remission, either temporary or permanent. And there is a spiritual healing or healing of the spirit, emotions or memories, which can be just as important as a physical healing even though it is not generally accepted as such.

When I had my healing from Marion, it brought about a physical remission which lasted many years. To me that was the important thing. But what in fact was more important, was the healing I began to receive when my cancer returned. That was the time for me to find peace and acceptance, which I finally did. As well, as you know, I needed very little morphine and was able to remain alert and in charge.

Sometimes an instant healing can take place, which often happens when there is the strong energy of a large gathering, for example in some of the churches that have healing services. The energy is very powerful when it comes from a large gathering. If the minister is a clear channel of healing and is sincere, it is akin to a huge voltage of energy being channelled through him, which brings healing and wholeness. Other cultures and religions also have healing rituals, which sometimes last for days. It is seen from here as a vortex of energy which is then directed to a particular person. Faith plays a great part, but is not always necessary. The fervent prayers of a few can bring about a miracle. In times of great need the angelic forces are brought into the situation.

Another type of help can come from actual treatments by medical people from here. Operations have been cancelled because suddenly a growth or a problem has disappeared between the taking of one x-ray and the next. This can be done in answer to a great need, in answer to a prayer, perhaps as a sign that spiritual help does exist or as a boost to faith, as the case may be. Many so-called miracles have occurred because of sincere prayer, although they are not always answered in the way expected or hoped for. Sometimes it is a case of being given the strength to cope, peace and acceptance, and an assurance that all will be well and that nothing happens unless it is God's will. Whenever people pray sincerely for others, there is great strength in it. Prayers for self, if not selfish, are just as beneficial.

The mechanics of the laying on of hands is the receiving of the divine healing power from God through another person. The word *channel* is a very good one. It is like electricity going through a wire to where it is needed. The electricity is there but it has to be put through wires before it can be used. Healing power is everywhere. The power of God is in and through everything but, according to the need, has to be channelled through a particular outlet. Whenever healing is accomplished, people say it is a miracle. Up to a point it is, but it is really available all the time.

Sometimes, even though healing is asked for, it is not what is wanted or needed at a soul level. Why did the person get the illness or problem in the first place? If negative feelings and emotions caused the illness, even if a healing appears to have taken place, the problem will recur. Even if a problem is cut out by surgery, the cure will not be permanent unless the cause of the problem no longer exists.

Then there are illnesses which are not easily remedied and it is time for the body to let go of this life. In these cases no amount of praying, laying on of hands, or other types of physical help will allow the life to continue.

Health

There is much written and spoken about health. Everyone wants a healthy body and most people try to maintain it in different ways. Some do all the wrong things, as if they do not care, but deep down it is natural to want to be healthy.

In these times it is becoming less easy to be healthy. Many problems have been accumulating on the planet, such as toxicity in the atmosphere, depletion of the ozone level and so on. Of course the rate of depletion of the forests and trees has had a huge effect not only on the rainfall but on the immune systems of mankind. The immune system of people is directly linked to the immune system of the planet, which is very badly affected by all the stress put on it from the ills I have mentioned. Health of course is not only affected by what is happening to the planet. Again, it is such an individual thing. There are some diets that are supposed to bring great benefits and, ultimately, perfect health. But no diet is right for every person, just as no medication, practitioner, or procedure is right for every patient. So for each person there is a different set of practices which is necessary to maintain or bring health.

There are many people suffering from allergies now, caused from a build up of toxins in the food, and from poisonous substances in the air, the water and the soil. These build ups suddenly become too much and a particular illness manifests; but not all people eating the same food become ill. Some have built up an immunity, as it were, while for others the food actually breaks down their immunity. Health is very much an individual pathway.

In the past, cholesterol has been seen as a major problem, but now it is no longer thought to represent the big threat that it once did. It really comes down to the fact that there is no general rule. Some people can have sweets and some must not, and the same applies to alcohol, coffee, meat and dairy products. They all suit some, and others have to be careful or abstain.

You remember your friend who was on such a strict diet for her cancer and was up at some unearthly hour to begin juicing her lettuce and other vegetables? As she said to you, 'There is that bloody Mark eating pies, cream cakes, tinned salmon and whatever else he fancies, and still he is in full remission.' I did too. And I certainly never went off meat. Mind you, I did eat more fruit and even had some salad; but I certainly was not obsessive about it. How I enjoyed our fish and chips every Friday. You made wonderful chips, Annie, and maybe the pleasure of eating them more than made up for the fat content because they brought me joy. After all, joy in life is a big help in maintaining health. How is that for justifying my eating habits!

When people become stressed and obsessive about diets and particular foods, it is not really helpful. In fact it is quite the opposite. By that I do not mean that it is better to eat what you like as long as it makes you happy; rather it is a case of moderation in all things - but obviously, if you are allergic to a particular thing, then it needs to be totally avoided.

A healthy mind and a healthy emotional life are very much a part of a healthy body. There is much written about the effects on the body of stress, anger, resentment, judgment and negativity. As I have mentioned before, these emotions are all seen in the aura, but then they move into the physical body with dire results. Even speaking of the past over and over without forgiveness or understanding finally tears away the protection, as it were, of the strength of the physical. It cannot be said often enough that forgiveness of the past, the people, the situation, and, most of all, yourself, is important. It is not just a spiritual law, it is a law that affects the physical body, and it carries great importance on this side as well.

Well, Annie, this is not a medical talk, but one I hope of common sense. It is interesting, is it not, to hear my ideas now of things to which I gave absolutely no thought or heed to when I was there? Well, my interests have changed dramatically and, as they say, 'Better late than never.'

Our Ideas Of Self

Some children feel that the love of their parents is conditional upon how they behave, so they try always to please their parents, disregarding their own inner feelings. This attitude can carry on into a marriage or relationship, or even a job or profession. When this happens the actual self-motivation is stifled and the person never rises to or wants a top position. These people are more comfortable deferring to a higher authority.

Then there is the situation where parents say that everything their children do is just wonderful - whether it is quite ordinary or extraordinary. The children then think they are great and better than others, and are shocked at school when they find they are not the most wonderful or the brightest. These children can then decide to become the best, or they can feel so deflated they do not even want to try. It is a difficult lesson to receive criticism and straight, honest opinions of work not well done after it has been *so* easy to receive praise. When children are brought up without love or appreciation, they may feel a total lack of self-esteem, or they can be determined to show that they can succeed, while always living with the hope of eventually receiving words of love and acceptance.

Some counselling sessions, courses and books suggest that an adult's problems are caused by his parents and his home life or lack of it. This is an easy way of explaining failure, lack of success or broken relationships. Individuals have to take responsibility for themselves rather than going through life blaming everybody and everything in the past for their lack of happiness.

To take responsibility for one's own success, one's own happiness, one's own life and whatever happens is a giant step forward. When I say 'whatever happens' I am speaking of events over which we have some control. There are things that occur that we are powerless to predict, let alone to stop.

A person's spiritual belief can be such a help and comfort when things happen over which they have no control. It may not make the situation easier to live through, but the feelings of total powerlessness and of the unfairness of life do not arise to make things even worse. To say 'I do not understand it, but obviously it is God's will,' does not bring quite the comfort desired. To say 'Oh well, I guess I deserved it from another life and it is my karma' is not much comfort either.

It is nearer the truth to think of God's will as being the creative force of harmony in all situations (even though this sounds a bit lofty and impersonal). As I see it, everything happens for a reason - not as a reward, not as a punishment, but as a lesson to give or a lesson to receive, or an experience to balance previous experiences. If we rape the Earth of so much natural food and cover and poison the waterways and oceans with our wastes, can we ask 'Why is God punishing us?' when great droughts and starvation occur. If you overeat, have no exercise, put on weight and get diabetes or arthritis, or both, it is not a punishment from God. I remember one of our friends saying to you after my death, 'It is hard to understand how God allowed something awful like that to happen to Mark.' Your reply which shocked him was, 'Well, he chain-smoked from the age of eighteen, so I do not think we can really blame God.' My word, Annie, that stopped the smiles for a while.

As we have free will much of the time, we can make it easier on ourselves by obeying the natural laws as much as possible. No one is perfect, for if we were, we would not need to be in a physical body. We can only do the best we can with what we come in with and what we are given to work with.

Where Is The World Going?

This question seems to be in people's minds now more than ever. There is so much uncertainty and fear, as if the most awful things are just around the corner. Everyone has to die, but life is continuous, so what is the problem about going somewhere that is safe from calamity? Death is just a going through to the real life, something to look forward to. Death is really living. The afterlife is really the afterdeath. In other words, life is the death and death is the real living. The thought of *how* the death will occur is the thing that causes the fear, but no amount of worry or concern will change it.

The type of death differs from country to country. Not many in the affluent countries die from disease and starvation. Not many in the poorer countries die from cancer and heart attacks caused by stress and being overweight. Each country has its particular difficulties. There is open warfare in some countries. In others it is a hidden warfare between the corrupt and the innocent, the drug pushers and the drug takers, the law enforcement agencies and the guilty. There is a kind of warfare in families, relationships, and firms with their bosses and workers. Children can be at war with their parents and teachers, and vice versa.

There is war and discord in every country and every walk of life; and in the midst of it are the peacemakers, those searching for a better way, those living a life of service and giving. The spiritual upliftment that the prayers of these people generate would amaze you. They not only help those for whom people have prayed, but those who have received the help are then able to support and help others. As a pebble thrown into a pool causes ever-widening ripples, so the upliftment and inspiration continue on to other people and situations. Never underestimate the power of even *one* prayer.

Also, be as helpful as you can wherever you can. This means showing kindness, giving encouragement, looking on the bright side and not holding grudges and recalling every last detail of past hurts and problems.

The Earth is in a state of great change. The theory of chaos before order is right. There is more chaos to come, but it will not be as drastic as some have prophesied. Their ideas of the Earth changes need never occur. When prophecies are made, people often take note only of the worst-case scenario. There is no point in conjecture. Only God knows. No matter what predictions are made about the future, things can always change as the result of prayer, a change of attitude and people taking responsibility for changing their own way of life.

Destiny And Free Will

Today I will speak about the tendency of those on Earth who expect that they will not die in a way that is *not* of divine authority.

First of all, death is set at the time of birth, but not because divine authority states that 'this is what you get'. Destiny and freewill are so intertwined that it is difficult to make a line of demarcation, as it were. Destiny is what *will* happen, but in a way, your destiny is what your freewill has dictated. How is that for a contradiction in terms?

When the soul has to return to the physical body, there are various options from which it has to choose in the way of parents, lifestyle, country and so on. These so-called freewill options are dictated by the lessons the soul needs to learn, so there is a boundary beyond which the choices may not be made. The boundary is made by *destiny*. Within that boundary, the length of life is set. The type of death is not always set, but if that is part of the lesson for the soul and those closely connected with it, then it is part of the destiny as well. For instance, my death was set, and within that time I had lessons to learn. Had I changed my attitudes, life-style and thinking, and had I learnt to give and to accept and communicate, then my quality of life, as well as yours, would have been different. As it was, I did not accept all the lessons. I had to learn the hard way - and so my illness and death were part of it. Mine was a destiny that could have been changed; but given my nature and behaviour, the chances of *not* having the hard lesson at the end would have been slim indeed. But then, as I have said before, such good has come even from that experience.

You have just heard of the tragedy of the death of your friend's eighteen-year-old only granddaughter. A death like that *is* a destiny. It is too much to do with timing and circumstances to be an accident. When the chance of it happening at all are so minimal, then it is fairly certain it is really meant to be. She felt nothing, and for her it was just a very quick return home again. For her sorrowing family and loved ones it is a very different thing. Can you imagine how a death - any death - affects people when there is so much love involved? Even where there is not as much love involved, the regrets, guilt and non-forgiveness all add up to a very difficult situation.

A death like that for no apparent reason creates so much sorrow. People ask 'Why should it happen to someone so young and lovely?' For people without a belief system there are no answers. For those with a religious or spiritual belief it highlights their own mortality and that of their children. It gives rise to deep thinking and wondering about life and death. On the positive side, it can encourage people to make the most of each day and not allow themselves to get caught up in minor problems and irritations.

Whenever these tragedies occur, there is a wave of great sorrow, anger and frustration. This is *not* helpful to the soul who has passed over, so it is doubly important for those with the understanding to pray for help and support for the soul and to ask for the Divine Light to surround it. It does anyway, but so much negativity coming from the Earth makes it less easy, as it were, to proceed on this side.

Sometimes the soul can become Earth bound, until the extreme grief and sorrow of their loved ones begin to ease. No matter how deep the sorrow, the understanding helps, but it does not take away the regrets, the grief, the memories of the joy shared, the dashed hopes for the future, and so on. Experiencing the grief and loneliness is a very natural process and needs to be worked through, but as is said at church services, 'we do not sorrow as those who have no hope'. That is the crux of the matter. There *is* hope, knowledge and belief which all help. A different type of grief is apparent with the death of a young person, a child or an infant because it seems that they have not had the opportunity of living a full life. If only people could understand the emptiness of life on Earth compared to the fullness of life here. It is really a little death on Earth and a long life here - a difficult concept to grasp for most people."

Some time later Mark wrote that what he had said about destiny being dictated by freewill required more explanation and continued:

"Destiny is what is absolutely set, even from before birth. Freewill is when there is a choice that can be made about a relationship, a job, a journey, where you live, where you move to, and so on. The choice is there regardless of whether your life is governed by a chosen framework of morals or not.

The time of death is set. Even in the case of war, murder, so-called accident and the big one of suicide, *there is no choice at all* as to the time. Perhaps the way in which death occurs can be changed if great changes have taken place within the self. If a man chooses not to fight in a war, then he obviously will not die from war injuries. Nevertheless, his time of death is set. Either he would not have died fighting, or he would die in some other way, depending on what his life span is. When a death is caused by a so-called freakish accident, not only the death, but also the type of death is fulfilling the destiny of the person.

When children have terminal illnesses and do symbolic drawings, it is quite obvious to those skilled in that area that the child knows *exactly* how long it will live, not on a conscious level but on a soul level. And when a treatment unexpectedly saves a life, the treatment itself is part of that person's destiny, which is *not* to die at that particular time.

If a couple meet, for example, in Europe while on a short holiday, and they come from opposite directions such as Australia and the United States, the meeting was in all probability the result of destiny.

Some marriages are a part of destiny and some are not. If a particular marriage brought a particular lesson, it might be said 'if only they had married so-and-so'. If they had, the lesson would still have been learnt, but in a different way, and maybe through a child rather than the spouse.

You all have guardians or guides from birth. It is their function to try to guide you through difficulties and to help in many situations. They never interfere with destiny or freewill. They can make the journey less difficult if you wish, but it is your free will that allows you to be open to their help. It is like deciding to take either the easy, smooth road to your destination, or the rough, rugged road. The analogy of the smooth road leading to hell and the rough road leading to heaven is not a good one. Many wrong decisions can lead to a very rough road indeed and appropriate actions and deeds can find a smooth road.

You have a saying about living each day as if it

will be your last, but planning as if you will live forever. This is not a bad philosophy to live by. What an incredible change there would be in the world if everyone thought like that. There would be no pollution or rape of the land, for who plans to live in a desert in the future or to have polluted air, water and food? And who would not be different if they knew they were living their last day on Earth? Of course not everyone would react to the latter idea in the same way, but most would probably live a better life for those precious hours.

The thing is, life is to be lived fully and richly, using all you have been given. To dwell on what you do *not* have is living very poorly indeed. There is no one on Earth who cannot find someone who is better off than they are, and others who are worse off. Who decides who is better off or worse off? Only the brief life span of now is seen and only the outer shell of the person. It is the real person inside, and the time that is not just a blink of the eye, but eternity, that is reality.

Every soul experiences what it needs. Destiny and freewill work together to make sure that occurs. To do the best you can in whatever you do is really all that is needed - and to ask forgiveness of yourself when you do not do your best. Ask forgiveness of others as well (and this can also include actions of making restitution in some way). All of this is freewill."

Giving To Self

After the school holidays had finished and I was alone once more I was happy to be able to write again.

(M): "Today is a new beginning for a new year of work and doing the best in every department; health, fitness, family, relationships, friendships and your work, which at present needs first priority. So off we go! What is our main responsibility? It is to Self, not anyone else. Does that come as a surprise? I have spoken of working on Self to get things right on the planet, but now I mean giving to Self.

There are those who think of getting everything for self regardless of anyone else. At the other end of the scale are the self-sacrificing people who think it is selfish not to think of others first - as mothers do for their children. Up to a point mothers do have to think of their children first, especially when they are quite young and unable to take care of their own needs. But there comes a time when a mother needs to realise that she is more than a mother or a wife. She is a unique child of God or the Universe with her own needs to be taken care of, and her own talents to be used. Some mothers get into such a rut of self-sacrifice they do not even recognise it. They feel the family should come first, but deep down they begin to resent the attitude of 'mother can do it' or 'mother will help'. It is a case of seeing clearly where there is a need and where there is a desire and to recognise the difference and act accordingly. A need and a desire can be the same thing and there is nothing wrong with that. A mother in particular needs to realise when it is appropriate for her to let her family go and think of what she would like to do for herself. If a mother's joy is to continue to care for her children and grandchildren to the exclusion of her own needs, that is her freewill choice. If this caring is done without joy, it is time for her to begin to evaluate her own personal needs. There will always be the self-sacrificing helpers and those who benefit from their selfless service without thought of giving in return. It is wise though to reflect on the karmic possibilities of 'as ye sow, so shall ye reap'."

Money

"Well Annie, what will we speak about today? Yesterday you suddenly thought of money, so perhaps we can say a bit about that. Almost everyone is concerned about it - the lack of it, how to have more, or how to make secure what is already owned.

When money is mentioned there is an instant reaction depending on people's attitude to it. When money is asked for, from here we can see who does not like giving and those who accept giving as part of receiving. Requests for very large amounts of money bring very large reactions, as it were.

Because of the way the economy of the world is handled, there are millions of people at almost starvation level, and some at starvation level, and yet there are many, many thousands who have so much wealth. There are also the comfortable in-betweens, who, compared to the very poor, have much more than is needed.

Whenever excess of wealth is put aside and not used, it is not doing any good at all. It should be used - not just invested to become a row of figures. So often money is just transferred from one column to another without actually producing anything but profit or loss. The economy is such a complex thing, not easily understood or explainable; but the way it is manipulated now is making the world a very unbalanced place as far as food and the necessities of life are concerned. You are aware of the inequalities that exist. There is no need to go into it. As you know, a number of what were thought to be very successful and wealthy men have been shown to be totally dishonest, causing losses of millions to average, hard-working people.

The Bible speaks of money. It is often misquoted as saying 'Money is the root of all evil'. It actually says that 'love of money is the root of all evil'. Well, I do not agree with that either. Possibly 'love of money is at the root of *much* evil' would be nearer to the way it is. God provides everything that is needed for the life and survival of the occupants of the planet, both human and animal. How many countries have no food at all; how many do not even bother harvesting what they grow, throw it away because the prices are too low, or have it stored away for the future. How can this be?

It Is Never Too Late - Chapter 3

Whenever there is a war or a calamity such as an earthquake, flood or hurricane, the amount of food and comforts that become available is amazing. No one goes without; but in so-called normal times, it is accepted that there are people who have no food or shelter. It is not even considered as a tragedy, as a desperate area of need.

As devastating as it is in war time, people share the little they have and care about their fellow beings; but when peacetime and prosperity come, it is back to 'everyone for themselves'.

If every person on the Earth gave, say, one tenth of what he or she had to someone with less, there would be no lack at all. Everyone would have enough. You would still have the very wealthy and the very poor, but there would not be death by starvation or lack of the minimum requirements for living. (That is something for you to think about - perhaps you will need a computer to prove or disprove that idea.)

Anyone who never gives at all, for whatever reason, has a karmic debt to pay, if not in this life, then in another. People place so much importance on their worldly goods - their homes, furnishings and possessions in general. One good heave of the earth's crust and it is all gone forever. A life lost is not lost. It goes on, but things cease to exist. They are totally unimportant to the extent that all energy and money and time are wasted if no other goals are sought. Knowledge and wisdom and expertise are never wasted and are carried on. Love, service, kindness, forgiveness and sharing are never wasted either and are really the 'riches' that should be worked for and *used* - not put away for a rainy day.

All of these thoughts and concepts may sound too lofty, too impractical. It is a case of little by little, day by day, when and where you are able. Not waiting until you have more than enough, but doing it *before* you have enough. And who says what enough is? The enough when we were children is not considered enough now. For the poorer countries, our enough then would be more than enough now. It would even be considered as wealth."

Channeling Or Mediumship

"Annie, today I am going to write about what is called *channeling* or *mediumship*. Either word is understood to be a description of the ability to receive messages or words of wisdom from the other side. These terms are used to explain what happens when some kind of contact is made with departed loved ones or other entities.

Just as there are many forms of mediumship, so are there different reasons for channeling. There are mediums who give personal messages about loved ones who have passed over and wish to contact those they have left behind. Through others come descriptions of their own passing and further experiences. Some give discourses which clarify the differences between spirituality and religious fervour. Others give encouragement and advice on how to live in a physical world, with all that this entails, without neglecting spiritual values. Mediums whose main object seems to be to give predictions about future events are much sought after.

Many of the well-known mediums communicate in what is known as 'deep trance'. In other words, their consciousness leaves their body and the body is then used by the communicating entity. The medium or channeller has absolutely no idea of what was said or what transpired. Sometimes the voice sounds similar to that of the medium, but the accent, intonation and way of expression do not. At other times the voice is entirely different. While in trance, these mediums can walk around with their eyes closed and interact with the people present in a normal manner.

Many mediums do not trance and are fully conscious of what they are saying. They repeat the words they are able to hear from the communicating entity. Other channellers are writers. They are used physically and their hand can work independently of their mind. This is known as automatic writing. There are people without any musical knowledge whatsoever who have received and recorded musical scores while fully conscious. Others can paint likenesses of the person communicating - sometimes a guide and often a loved one. To see a drawing made of a departed loved one, quite unknown to the artist, can have a great impact, as you can imagine.

Being a channel is not a talent everyone has. It is

not like intuition or a psychic ability. Most people have these to some degree (some to almost a minus degree), and others a very high plus. These abilities can be developed and many psychics have worked hard at developing their gifts. The word *psychic* often has a negative connotation, but it is in fact a natural God-given gift that can be very apparent, or can be unused and unnoticed. Channeling is different; it can be worked on and developed if the gift already exists, but it is not something you can learn to do (like telepathy, for instance). Some who channel have done it in many life times and it is just second nature to them. Others have it lying dormant until circumstances bring it to the fore.

Being a medium is not an easy job. Even for a gifted and highly qualified medium, with much experience and knowledge brought from a past life, it is still a very difficult pathway to follow. Used honestly and sincerely it means a lifetime of responsibility, giving without thought of personal gain, and being at the beck and call of everyone in need. When born into a family that is totally ignorant of such things, it can be a very hard life for the medium until they are old enough to break away from the home environment. It seems that many people with an exceptional gift of mediumship *do* have very difficult lives, which gives them understanding and compassion and a great desire to help those in need. There are others who succumb to the temptation of being feted and sought after, and paid handsomely for their readings, books and lectures. There are, however, many communications that are not of a good or high order, and much wrong information is fed to people who are searching for spiritual truths. As you know, people do not change their basic characteristics when they come here, and if they are ego-centred and love to dominate, what better way than to become a guide to some similarly oriented person. Suddenly a fantastic guide or master is channeling all kinds of misinformation, beautifully expressed in words and sentences that sound 'spiritual'. The channels themselves find notoriety and money, and have gullible people hanging on their every word and paying good money to hear the nonsense that is spoken. There are many who have gone along this path and no real harm comes from it - just misinformation, perhaps resulting in wrong decisions and actions. When channeling is done for self-gratification or ego only, or to make money, it is of a different quality. There is not the help given from here.

Mediums who charge enormous fees are often doing the work for that reason alone, and soon the purity of the channel can become clouded, as it were. This is not to say that financial gain is not appropriate. The gift is from God, but the time given is from the channeller. If they devote their time to helping people rather than working at a paying job, then is it totally appropriate to charge a fee. What may be thought by some to be excessive charges may be to make up for those who do not or cannot pay the prescribed fee. It is up to those seeking help to take responsibility in this matter. The channeller helps where it is necessary, without the thought of payment being the main consideration.

Many people are more concerned about predictions for the future than with spiritual truths, about how best to live their life on Earth, or how to be more prepared for life on the other side. Some predictions *do* come true, but very often they *do not*. Unless it is of real help to know of the future, and only God knows everything about the future, then predictions are a guide post only and often do not point in the right direction anyway. So many mistakes have been made because of a prediction which then did not occur. As long as people have freewill they can change much of what is seen as a future happening. If everything goes on in the same way as it was when the prediction was made, then it might happen; but so often it does not. The whole world is in a state of change. Some things are inevitable; death certainly is, but that is the one thing not usually given to mediums to predict. Sometimes people have a knowing of their own impending death or even that of a loved one. That is different to being told by someone else. A dream of death rarely means a literal death. It usually means a big change in lifestyle, attitudes or circumstances.

When people want something, or hope for a particular thing to happen, it can actually be seen in the aura surrounding the person, like a 'thought form'. From here it is difficult to know then, if it will occur. That is why so *many* personal questions about the

It Is Never Too Late - Chapter 3

future receive the wrong answer. The hope or even the fear surrounding the inquirer can be seen from here, and this is then channeled through the psychic. Sometimes a strong thought is picked up telepathically by the medium and the prediction is not really channelled at all. The whole matter of channeling is all very complex and is fraught with difficulties. The thing is *not to* take it all too seriously until the actual information has proven itself or feels very right. It is not showing lack of faith to query or question, or even disbelieve. It is much healthier than just accepting every word as truth and infallible wisdom. That is when problems arise.

It is the medium's job to channel as it is given and to put aside, as it were, any thoughts, queries and doubts. Otherwise, it is a very difficult job from here. Once the channeling is complete, it is quite appropriate to doubt and query and *then* to ask questions so the more perplexing issues can be clarified."

Temper

One morning I had become very angry about the contents of a letter I had received. I rang the writer and in no uncertain terms set straight what I saw had been a totally incorrect assumption.

(M): "Well now, what can we speak about today? Perhaps *bad temper* would be appropriate. My word, you *were* upset. We could see the lights flashing and were fascinated because your aura does not often look like that. The sudden flare up of anger is different to the type of slow, steady anger that can be felt in a family or work situation that builds up over a long period of time. That shows black and red in the aura as well, but it is not as alive. It is more like a smouldering fire as compared to a roaring flame; but roaring flames usually disappear more quickly than a steady burning log, for example. The quick anger which soon expires is *much* more preferable than the feelings of anger, disappointment and resentment that continue.

Really bad temper or bad moods can make everyone suffer. It is very uncomfortable for others and if they in turn become angry or depressed, then it is not good for anyone. The *original* bad-tempered person has a lot to answer for. First of all, their own wellbeing is badly affected. Then those contacted are affected. Then, if they allow it to happen, others can be affected physically, and thirdly it gives even more negative vibrations to the planet as a whole. These negative vibrations accumulate and the final scenario can be wars and catastrophes. It sounds very extreme, but that is the way it goes. Volcanoes and earthquakes are very much linked to the people on the planet. When people's emotions are full of hatred, anger, revenge and other extreme negativity, the whole delicate balance of the planet is affected. If only people realised it and lived accordingly.

Well Annie, you did not expect your anger this morning to inspire such a talk. See how good can come from any situation - even temper? But it is better not to have it in the first place, even when feeling totally justified. You could have rung with the same message but without the emotion, which in turn upset the person you rang. Who knows how many people she then upset with the feelings she received from you?"

Expectations

"When people go over to the other side they always take with them their thought forms of what it is going to be like, though not always on a conscious level, of course. These thought forms may be brought through from childhood, from something someone has said, or even a book they have read. Some people do not have any conscious ideas about it at all and yet they find their loved ones waiting to greet them - if they have retained some feelings for them.

There are always beings of light or angels, but not everyone can see them. When a person has a great fear of what it is like to die, it is as if a thick cloud wraps around them, and more work - if you can call it that - is needed to help them lose the fear and see the beauty and feel the peace as they arrive.

Not many know what to expect. They hope for the best, but there is a lingering doubt which so often comes from a feeling of guilt about the life they have led. Some people with a very firm religious background which had strict rules of conduct and not much freedom of expression are very sure they will be in heaven if they have kept the rules they were told were most important for their spiritual welfare. They come to the time of remembering and regrets, just as everyone else has to, and they may find those particular rules were not important.

When people have some idea of what to expect, they move forward quickly. As I told you, I had no fear of death and welcomed it as an end to my illness and inability to live as I wanted. I also had listened to your many discussions with others about your beliefs and what you were learning. I had no barriers of strict beliefs to break through. Followers of other great religions have different experiences. You are familiar with the verse 'In my Father's house are many mansions', and so it is. All races, creeds and cultures have their own mansion as it were, built by their particular belief, background and expectations. Expectations not clearly felt or thought about are soon able to be changed to how it really is. When I say how it really is, again I remind you that it is different for each soul as there are so many factors involved.

But let us take the case of a very ambitious businessman who lived for his work and did what he wanted to make life as pleasurable as he could for himself, without too much regard for anyone else. (Does that sound familiar Annie?) Well, in my case, if I had died suddenly in the midst of my importance and ego and selfishness, I would have experienced much more difficulty than I did. I would have been so angry at having died before I felt I should have. I would have been aggressive and difficult and also wanted a smoke and a drink constantly. I could have had them, but they would not have brought any relief at all. It would have taken time for me to be open enough to receive the love and teaching and comfort that is available. Maybe I would not have seen or acknowledged my parents. It is a very complex thing to explain, but a strong determined mind makes great difficulties.

A long illness is seen as a tragedy and a sudden death is thought to be preferable for the person concerned. But this may not be the real picture. My illness was a blessing for me, as I found peace and acceptance before I came over. It was not much fun for you, but on another level you gained great strength and understanding. And look what we are doing now. You still have difficulty accepting it all, as if it is just too good to be true.

I have implied that people experience, more or less, what they expect, but that is not exactly the way it is either. Many people have no expectations and no interest whatsoever in advancing spiritually. And if this is the case, they can live a life very much like the one they experienced on Earth. They find eventually that they can build what they wish from their thoughts, like a home, garden and so on, and that is what they do. They build a home like the one they left, or if they are into house-planning, they build a dream home and wait for their spouse or family to arrive. Meanwhile, they may take up a hobby they always wished to do or one they already enjoyed doing. They can remain in a

It Is Never Too Late - Chapter 3

situation like this for a very long time. Eventually it is time for them to return for another term on Earth. Then the teachers or helpers begin their work. They visit, as it were, and the situation is clearly explained. Of course many do not want to return, but after more explanations and discussion, they may begin to accept the situation. They may be shown their options and what they need to learn. The teachers help them to decide and it is lovingly and gently done. If they still refuse to return, they can, on occasions, be allowed to stay. They may eventually decide to return to Earth to meet with a spouse or loved one.

Sometimes souls *need* to return for a particular reason, whether they want to or not, and this is where freewill does *not* play a very big part in the decision. Everything is done for the highest good of all and no mistakes are made. The souls who did not want to go in the first place may then decide to abort or miscarry, or to leave at birth or soon after. Not all lives are set from birth to death, as I keep saying. In the case of young bodies, there can be a change of direction. When a small baby dies, it is not always a case of them changing their mind. It may be exactly the way it was meant to be for the parent's learning. Even the medical staff can learn great lessons, which may benefit others. Many so-called cot deaths bring about a new understanding that helps countless numbers in the future. No happening is ever wasted. It is all part of divine planning, which is more complex than words can describe or minds can comprehend.

Perception and Interpretation

People's interpretation of things they see or hear depends upon their perception, and this varies from person to person. Each person in a group of people watching a particular happening would recount what they saw quite differently. Perception can be coloured by what a person believes or wants to believe, by the circumstance, or to whom they are telling the story. The reasons are as endless, as are the interpretations.

People have selective memories. When attending a lecture or talk, if the subject matter discussed or facts given are what the listener already believes, there are no problems of recall. If the facts are entirely new but compatible with the person's ideas, they are retained easily. If they are totally against a person's intellectual reasoning or moral values, they may be remembered because of the negative impact they made, or they may be totally erased from the memory. For instance, in the case of a discussion on life after death, if what is said follows the listeners' belief systems, it will inspire and elate. If on the other hand it is contrary to their beliefs, then they will be appalled at what they consider to be false teachings and will not be influenced at all, except, perhaps, to then search for affirmation of the belief they hold so dear.

As has been explained, people with very strong beliefs of how things will be in the afterlife, build their own reality here. Some churches still have their congregations of believers who stay in that group for

It Is Never Too Late - Chapter 3

a long time. It takes a gradual and sometimes lengthy process to move these people towards a fuller understanding. This can also explain the different channeling experiences that occur.

A person who has always been taught that reincarnation is a false and dangerous teaching may not let go of that belief for a long time. So if that person was channeling, they would not mention reincarnation. It would not yet be in their belief system, and in fact may have no relevance to the message they wished to give. If the people receiving the channeling also had no belief in reincarnation, then the very mention of it may take away their acceptance of the message that there is life after death, and that there is total love and non-judgment waiting. The perception of the afterlife varies here just as beliefs and interpretations vary on Earth. There is one experience, however that all must go through, whether it is their belief or not, and that is the self-judgment or the regretting.

Now we come to interpretation. In every religion there are many interpretations of the 'truth', which lead to the formation of extremist groups, as well as groups of more liberal thinkers. The truth of the Bible is often mentioned, but who has the *true interpretation?* A comma in a particular place can change the whole meaning of the message. Do you remember listening to a discussion about whether a person went to heaven or hell immediately on death, or whether they slept in the grave until the day of resurrection? The 'heaven or hell immediately' belief was justified by Jesus' words to the thief on the cross: 'I say unto you, today thou shalt be with me in paradise.' The other interpretation was explained by the comma being placed *after* 'today': 'I say unto you today, thou shalt be with me in paradise.' So two entirely different beliefs are formed because of the placing of a comma. Heated arguments can result, without a possible conclusion.

Because the events recorded in the Bible were written so long after the actual events, and later the different languages were translated into one language, you can imagine the room for error. In the new version of the St. James Bible, the word *unicorn* was replaced by 'wild ox' - quite a difference. But it is totally unimportant to the wonderful thread of truth that runs throughout the Bible, and dissecting it all on a historical, logical or theological basis does not add to the truth at all. In fact, all religions have beautiful spiritual truths, but they are often altered or covered by particular interpretations.

Nowadays there is a tendency to disagree about whether Jesus actually died on the cross and was raised from the dead. Some like to believe he lived for many years, travelling the world and visiting other countries. Many cultures do have accounts of a holy man who healed the sick and raised the dead. Some say that the dead who were given life by Jesus were only in a coma, and that his miracles were more or less imaginings and false writing to make him appear more special. The thing of importance is the message he gave of love, service, forgiveness and non-judgment of one's neighbour. It is his life that is the thing to concentrate on rather than his suffering and death. But certainly, dying and then being seen by so many, gives the hope of life after death.

Even the meaning of the sacraments differs widely from church to church. The interpretation of what was divinely commanded in regard to the Lord's Supper, baptism and marriage has caused wide and often bitter dissension. The New Testament was written long after Jesus' death, and memory is a strange thing, as I have pointed out elsewhere - quite selective to suit the occasion. Again, it is not important. Will a God of love punish people because they interpreted His words in a particular way and it was not what He meant?

If you consider that every soul at some time has belonged to most religions, there is no point in being judgmental and intolerant about any belief.

Right And Wrong

The judgment of what is right and wrong differs vastly from person to person and from country to country. What is right in one culture is wrong in another. It is wise to accept what feels absolutely right within you, unless it brings hurt or harm to another. That is where the still small voice comes in. The conscience is our higher Self speaking to us, but sometimes it is so covered with layers of false living, denial and conditioning that it is not heard. You can only live in the way you feel is right and do the best you can. Be sure that it is what you *feel* is right and not simply what has been drummed into you. Many go through life feeling guilty all the time, and it is because of their background and upbringing. You need to think about *why* something is wrong, *who* told you so, and *what* the results of the action will be?

From here, we see so much guilt causing havoc in relationships, family life and the religious life. Anything that harms anyone, especially if done deliberately, is of course not right; but sometimes things are done unknowingly or without realising what the results will be, and that is different.

Certainly, if the ten commandments were followed to the best of everyone's ability, the world would be a much better place. The two commandments that Jesus gave, 'Love thy God' and 'Love thy neighbour', embody everything given in the ten commandments. Trying to live by them is the highest and best that anyone can do. On many occasions, knowing whether something is right or wrong may be an easy, clear decision; but often what is a right or wrong action can be clouded by circumstances. Other countries, cultures and religions may have customs and beliefs you think are archaic and perhaps horrifying. And they may consider that what *you* do is equally wrong and against the laws of God.

Be careful not to make judgmental comments. What you consider to be right can be considered totally wrong by someone else.

Scientific Breakthroughs

There is much written about the equality of the sexes. Up to a point that is as it should be. But there are differences apart from the obvious ones as far as the physical bodies are concerned. The brain *is* different for males and females and the amount of male and female hormones play an important part. There are hereditary factors also and upbringing plays a role, but generally speaking males and females do have different aptitudes. Although because generalisations do not ever apply to the whole picture, all along the line, as it were, you have exceptions to the rule. The thing to do is to be thankful for the talents and gifts you have, whether being of male or female gender, and use them to the best of your ability.

There is a lot of nonsense in a way, about scientifically proving which things men are better at, and which things women do best, and it does not help life as it is to be lived. Any breakthrough in any field of endeavour eventually helps the planet in some way. There are many pressing problems that elude the grasp of people. Whenever the planet enters a really bad time, it is then that great breakthroughs are made. It is as if the urgency makes people more open to the guidance that is *always* available but so often not used or even noticed.

The help from here is intensified the more in need an area of endeavour is, whether it is medical, scientific or the ills of the planet needing to be redressed.

Not just anyone can pick up the ideas and put them to work; it has to be someone who is very knowledgeable about, and actually working in the area where help is required. For example, you would not have a doctor or a technician in a medical laboratory suddenly approaching a problem to do with toxicity or the depletion of the ozone level; and you would not find a problem about physical disease being solved by an engineer. Guidance is given to someone who has already been working diligently in the particular field and who has given much thought and work to the solving of the problem. This narrows the field quite a lot. There are many problems and a large population, but very few suitable channels who are able to receive the inspiration and work it through.

There comes a point where a big breakthrough has to be made for the overall good of humanity. Then it appears. There is always the hope and expectation that the power from this side will overcome the ills of the Earth. But who decides what are ills and what are not? Difficult situations can be very much what is needed on some level. So that is not very positive, is it? It comes down to having faith that everything is as it should be - not an easy thing to accept or believe when one sees warfare, starvation and suffering.

Let us move to a more hopeful note. When you pray for the Divine Light to surround someone or something or some area or work, or anything, it *always* helps. There is *never* a time when it does not. So once again, never neglect prayers for anything, anyone or any situation that you feel is in need of help. The Great Invocation as you know is a very powerful prayer for all humanity, but every personal prayer, no matter how simple or brief, also brings help.

Meditation

When people meditate they move into another dimension. There are many types of meditation and some are complex and difficult to do, but anyone can meditate in some form or another. The way you were introduced to it (sitting quietly and visualising the colours of the rainbow) is excellent. Most people are able to do this, and if they never go beyond that, it does not matter. It just stills their mind for that time. Working in a garden or gazing at a beautiful scene can be very quietening to the mind also. When the mind is still and free from worry and concern, the body has time to heal.

Relaxing is not the same as meditating and stilling the mind. Relaxing is resting the body, but the mind can keep on worrying and thinking and planning. Relaxing the body is not as important, restful or healing as relaxing the mind. When you are meditating, we see what you are visualising and it is lovely to see. We see the change in your aura and your energy. *Never* underestimate the power of meditation.

While the power of meditation is within and surrounding the person, the power of prayer is quite different. It goes beyond the person, and even if the prayer is for yourself, it usually involves others in some way. If you pray for good health, for success in a project, or for wisdom or patience, it certainly involves others. The saying that 'no man is an island unto himself' is so right - everything said, done or thought has a reaction and goes out into the space of others as well."

Illusion

"Today I will speak to you about the reality of the universe. How is that for a profound title? You are laughing, and why not?

There is much written about how everything is an illusion and does not really exist. When you burn your finger on a hot stove it is difficult to accept that it is merely an illusion and did not happen. Material things *do* exist and happenings *do* happen, but what is illusion is how we *react* to what happens or what is.

Our illusions are what we allow ourselves to feel or how we think things are. For instance, if you see a person as kind, loving, wonderful, and so on, that is your illusion. They may be like that, but how do you know what is the reality? When you see someone who is mean, nasty, vindictive and acting very much against your ideas of how they should be, then that also is an illusion. How you perceive happenings and people's actions are illusions.

Another example is the suffering in different countries. What you see as a tragedy, a terrible happening, something that should not be allowed to go on, may not be that way at all. It is the illusion that comes from our understanding and our background.

This is a very difficult thing to explain. Pain can be an illusion. One person has a problem and perhaps sees it as a discomfort. Another person with a similar problem sees it as a situation giving much pain and it is felt as pain. Some illnesses are, as you know, caused by thought. The thought is the illusion but the physical manifestation is not an illusion. The pain really exists. Pain, and extreme pain at that, can be caused by illusions; but it can also be caused by an actual physical injury. The injury is not an illusion but the pain can be.

The Way People View Their Lives

Every person's path is different. No two are alike and that is how it is. No two people are the same or even similar. No matter how alike identical twins are, they each have a separate soul and they have had separate lives over and over.

Many people view their lives as being unlucky, unfortunate or not in any shape or form as they would have wished. In fact, every person is just where he or she is meant to be, and even the experiences are more or less similar to what was needed.. The less important events in your life, however, can be altered, for everyone has freewill. When it comes to your birth, your parents, the country where you were born, well, that is the way it was meant to be.

Unfortunately, so many bewail and bemoan that they were born at all, and as for their misfortune in having parents like they have, well, it is all just too unfortunate. But you choose your own parents. At least, you know who they will be and the reason they are the ones. You are made aware of the lessons and experiences you need to have and there can be a choice of a number of parents. If your lesson is to use wealth and power wisely, then it is unlikely you will choose poverty stricken parents in a slum somewhere. If you have abused wealth and power and need to learn what it is like to be in need and perhaps what it is like to be badly treated because you are in a powerless position, then you will not, in all probability, choose a high quality lifestyle with luxury at every turn.

Those are two extremes. In between, you have a great variety of situations. Some wonderfully gifted musicians are born into families in which musical ability has been part of the family background for generations and, in that case, everyone thinks their abilities have been inherited. Then you have a family in which there has never been any artistic talent or even a liking for it - and along comes a child who seems to belong to someone else. They look different, they seem different and they have incredible talent. To succeed, that child has to surmount unimaginable odds.

You need to see your life as an opportunity to learn and to come nearer to whatever it is you are trying to accomplish. Some children need a lot of encouragement to succeed. Others succeed because they received no encouragement and their determination pushed them along. Some people who encounter lots of stumbling blocks give up and think how badly they are done by. Others see the opportunities around them to overcome the problems.

There are no exact answers or general rules in the game of life. Someone who is going to perfect a marvellous invention to help humankind will not be born in the wilds of a jungle somewhere. And so it goes. It is all a marvel of cause and effect, free will and destiny, and karma. Every life is precious and has its value and its use and no one has ever been born or died that has lived and died for nothing - no matter how it may appear.

Power Of Thoughts

There is much said about the power of positive thinking, and it is powerful. But what about negative thinking? Negative thinking has as much power but in a totally destructive way. Positive thinking brings improvement in health, relationships, achievements and so on. Negative thinking not only negates improvement, but results in even less of what is wanted and needed. To always see the worst in any situation is very destructive to the person who sees, thinks and talks about it, as well as to the situation itself. Acceptance of what one cannot change is very worthwhile. As said in the prayer of St. Francis, 'God grant me the serenity to accept the things I cannot change, the courage to change the things I can, and the wisdom to know the difference'. I actually copied those words from a card you had on your desk and kept them in a book in my office. It was during a particularly difficult time for me, which again I did not let on about. I always had to be the invincible one, showing no fears or weakness."

When Two Loves Are Waiting, What Then?

A friend had been speaking to me about a concern she had about arriving on the other side and finding both of her 'true loves' waiting for her. She wondered how it would be, how they would act, and with whom would she spend her time. To my surprise, the next time Mark communicated, not only did he comment on her concerns, but wrote about them at some length.

(M): "And now I have something for your friend. She mentioned a few times the situation of having two dearly loved people here and wondered what would happen when she comes over - who will she be with?

There are many cases where there have been two real loves as you yourself have experienced - and some have even more than two on occasions - ha! No matter how deep each love has been, they are NOT the same. Physical attraction and interests on a mind or soul level may be similar, but they may also be quite different. The actual feeling of oneness and the quality of time spent together can be similar but never the same. Over here, the time spent with others has to do with many areas. There is never the feeling of possessiveness or having to be together, no matter what the circumstances were on Earth. Each person is allowed or has the freedom to be who and what they are. They can go where they want to and follow the interests they have a feeling for. There is not the thing of 'Oh well, I'll go with you to please you and then you can do the same for me'. That is the way of living together on Earth - wishing to please the person one loves and fitting in with each other's lives. Here it is quite different. Each person has total space and freedom and no one here needs anyone to make their life complete or better. This is not to say that life here is not enhanced by the company of a much loved companion, but unless it is harmonious in every facet then it does not exist all the time. It is a coming together in some areas and moving apart in others.

For instance, your friend will naturally share many interests with her first husband as she did during their very happy marriage. Her relationship with her second partner was based on interests which were very much a part of her work and which had not been shared by her husband. Here she can share these with her second partner and extend her knowledge in them. In between she may learn and experience with others she has loved during other times. There are no ill-feelings or jealousies harboured, because there is such complete understanding on every level here about those with whom you have been on Earth.

This does not happen in an instant as you know. It is a process that for some is lengthier than others. But in the case of a person who has two loved ones waiting on this side, they have gained knowledge and understanding and do not expect their newly arrived loved one to choose between them. There would be no jealousy or rivalry involved but only joy, peace and harmony. Of course, they may not both be waiting. One may have already returned to Earth, but this is unusual unless a great length of time has elapsed since their death.

In our earlier communications, Annie, you commented once that the gods must laugh at our goings-on, especially at our incredible egos. At the time my answer was, 'Annie, they neither laugh nor cry - they just love and understand.' I think that would explain exactly the attitude of your friend's two loves - they will love and understand."

Mark's Conclusion

"Annie, today I shall round off what I have written to you. So many words and so many subjects, and many of them a surprise to you. They are my thoughts, ideas, perceptions and what I have learned so far as I have experienced them.

Everyone's experiences are not identical, as I have told you; the number of different experiences equals as many individuals as have existed on Earth. Naturally, many are similar, but no two are the same.

Much is written of near death experiences and these are very comforting to those who accept them. But of course, a near death experience is not the same as an actual death experience. It gives the knowledge that there *is* a life after death and that there is love and a non-judgmental welcome awaiting. That is not all that life after death is. Death is like opening a door to your crop of fine golden wheat. In other words, what you have sowed in your life is fully grown and waiting to be harvested - *and only you can harvest it.*

I have written what I have because it is important for those who are left behind to know that after death their loved ones are not only aware of what they did during their lives, but they realise why the ones they have left acted as they did. If you could only see as we can, the grief and regrets, the resentments, guilt and non-forgiveness so often felt by the bereaved, you would realise how important it is to forgive both yourself and the one who has gone. Here we gain an understanding of our family and friends' feelings and their past actions, and we realise why things were as they were.

It is important to understand how much the person who has died needs your love, your forgiveness and your prayers. When I say prayers, I mean even just thoughts of wishing the person well in their new life.

When I came over, I felt your love, forgiveness and understanding, and you cannot imagine how that helped me. It is as if the ties that bind are broken and one is free to move on. When there is deep grief, regrets, guilt and a rehashing of all the negative areas of a relationship, it is very difficult to move on to where the forgiveness and freedom from regrets allows one to be. This does not mean that the negative areas are forgotten; they are there in the memory, but without bitterness and emotion. I have mentioned these truths often throughout this collection of my thoughts, but I cannot stress the importance of it all too much.

Forgiveness can begin before a parting. Whenever you feel you have hurt someone by word, thought or deed, it is helpful to say in your mind - and *mean* it - 'forgive me for that thought, word or deed'. When possible, it is helpful to say to the person 'I am sorry'. You were always good at that, but for me it was almost impossible. Forgiveness has nothing to do with thinking over and over, 'If only I had...' That sort of regret is difficult to cope with, both there and here. It is a matter of letting go, of accepting that there is now a total understanding - and so why regret and wish things had been different? It does no good at all and hinders both parties.

If things are such that they need to be worked through in another life, they will be and that is all part of the laws of life. The intricacy and complexities, as I have said, cannot be even vaguely imagined. Where I am now is really the kindergarten stage, as far as learning, experience and knowledge are concerned, but it is still a far cry from where I was when I was with you, Annie. Without a doubt we have both been very blessed by the interaction we have had since my departure. When we were together, could you have imagined a more remote possibility than a communication developing from me to you, from this world to yours? Even with your beliefs you would never have imagined such a thing. But stranger things happen all the time. They are called *miracles*.

Well Annie, this is all I am going to write to you with regard to this book. I wish you and all the readers many blessings and a wider understanding of how things can be. Death is *not* the closing of a door emblazoned with the words 'It is too late'. It is an open pathway to greater understanding, forgiveness and an opportunity for a further and happier life - life here and life there. Here and there are not even a breath apart and are inextricably bound together. All my love always - Mark."

It Is Never Too Late - Chapter 3

My Conclusion

Many letters and cards arrived after Mark's death, some of which were unexpected. Members of the church I once belonged to wrote and rang as did people Mark had worked with. However, there was one card that had a profound effect on me. It was from the matron of the hospice where Mark had died. It was penned beautifully in calligraphy, black ink on white parchment.

Anne:
If I should die and leave you here awhile,
be not like others sore, undone who keep
long vigils by the silent dust and weep.
For my sake turn again to life and smile,
nerving thy heart and trembling hand to do
something to comfort other hearts than thine.
Complete these dear unfinished tasks of mine,
and I, perchance, may therein comfort you.
Anon.

As I read this, the floodgates finally opened and I sobbed for I don't know how long. It was not so much that I was moved by the sentiments expressed by a loving husband to help and comfort his grieving wife. Rather, it was that I was plunged into the depths of sorrow and regret because nothing - no time or experience - in our marriage could have generated such thoughts. That was then. Now the words seem to aptly express the feelings of the Mark I have come to know. I can recall aspects of our marriage without the anger, resentment and guilt I had always felt, and in fact it seems as if they belonged to someone else's experiences, not mine.

Through these communications, I have not only gained an understanding of life on the *other side* but also an acceptance of life here. The Mark I knew no longer exists. He is now without all the layers of personality that he needed for this time with me. And what inexpressible comfort it is to know that he has such an understanding of the person I was when I was with him and that he forgives me. We each played our part, and as Mark once wrote, 'not always in a way to be recommended'.

Mark and I have completed our work together in a most unexpected way and now Mark can move on to where he needs to be to learn and experience more. I know I am never alone, as everyone on Earth is cared for and guided by their helpers, but, as Mark has said, the help and guidance needs to be acknowledged and accepted. This clarifies and strengthens what is given.

When Mark began to communicate we were both beginners, and now Mark has completed his studies with the class and I am still in it. Some day we will be able to laugh together even more, as we recall the interactions during our marriage with further understanding. Until that time I will always be grateful for the miracle Mark and I experienced - not only the communication that took place, but the love, understanding, help and knowledge I received. I now pass it on to you.

It Is Never Too Late - Chapter 3

THE GREAT INVOCATION

From the point of light within the mind of God
let light stream forth into the minds of men.
Let light descend on Earth.

From the point of love within the heart of God
let love stream forth into the hearts of men.
May Christ return to Earth.

From the centre where the will of God is known
let purpose guide the little wills of men -
the purpose which the masters know and serve.

From the centre which we call the race of men
let the plan of love and light work out
And may it seal the door where evil dwells.

Let light and love and power restore the plan on Earth.

WORLD GOODWILL
International Headquarters
3 Whitehall Court
LONDON SW1A 2EF, UK

Other compatible books by Triad include:

GOD I AM - From Tragic To Magic
by Peter O. Erbe

There is a silent aching in the human soul for hope and joy, a void that longs to be filled. Hope is expectancy for something to come. To go beyond hope, to arrive at what we hope for - to lift the soul from the dense clouds of turmoil, sorrow and stagnation to the heights of clarity into light and Love - is our purpose here. This message tears the veil of make-believe and reveals our time, against all appearances, as the most exciting to be in. It inspires the soul to soar again - to release itself into freedom, the ongoing adventure of Spirit where all things are made new.

ISBN: 0 646 05255 1, size A5, 250 pages, soft cover.

P'TAAH - AN ACT OF FAITH
channeled by Jani King

P'taah, a Pleiadean energy, tells of the grand changes to come for humanity and the planet Earth. He opens our vista to a universe teeming with life. He speaks of the inner earth people and the star-people and in doing so, assures us that we are not alone. What is more, he presents us with the panacea to transmute fear into love, to discover who we really are. Gently he dissolves the imprisoning shackles of dogma and concept, which lock Man into a consciousness of survival thinking, and reveals, contrary to all appearances, an irresistible, breathtakingly beautiful destiny for Mankind.

The love of the star-people for humanity could not be expressed any better than in P'taah's own words: We will do anything to bring you home!

ISBN: 0 646 07469 5, size A5, 252 pages, soft cover.

P'TAAH - TRANSFORMATION OF THE SPECIES
channeled by Jani King

In an evermore troubled world, P'taah's message creates a light beacon signalling the end of humanity's long tunnel of darkness, leading it into light and joy.

Excerpt: 'You will come into concepts beyond imagination. When you come into the knowing that there is no separation of anything, then indeed you will change the universe. Grand times of illumination, until there will be no time when you will not know that you are truly God.

And when that time comes, beloved ones, your planet will reflect lights beyond imaginings - rainbow hues dancing like a fireworks display to light up the galaxies. The planet indeed will be a reflection of the GOD I AM.'

ISBN: 0 646 13606 2, size A5, 252 pages, soft cover.

ST. GERMAIN - EARTH'S BIRTH CHANGES
channeled by Azena

The upheavals, the unrest and torment within humanity at this time are the contractions and labour pains heralding a birth of an incomprehensible, cosmic magnitude. Earth and her children, in unison with the Solar System and thousands of galaxies, are birthing into a new dimension. From the shores of eternal being, from the Council of Light, comes one called St. Germain to assist in this birthing process. As he bares his heart in love and compassion, rekindling an ancient memory, he transforms the prophecies of Old, of looming calamities and trepidation, into shining, new horizons without circumference. His gift to us is not approximate statement, but the promise of fact: freedom for humanity.

ISBN: 0 646 21388 1, size A5, 280 pages, soft cover.

window in the night with candles alight, beckoning, and knows with trembling heart his kin await him with open loving arms; and no greater the anguish of his yearning than in this final hour before his return.

Take comfort then - for truly, the journey is but over. As in the blink of an eye shall you awaken and naught shall remain but the fleeting memory of an impossible dream.'

ISBN: 0 9586707 0 6, size 11.5 x 17.5 cm, 165 pages, s/cover.

ST. GERMAIN - TWIN SOULS & SOULMATES
channeled by Claire Heartsong and Azena

'Experiencing Christ-consciousness within yourself, loving unconditionally that which you are as you exist and abide in your reality at this point in time, creates the resonance within your being which attracts the identical essence within the opposite body of soul energy - your soulmate will manifest in physicality as a natural progression and merges with your energy and you with it. And as you merge together closer and closer and drink more and more of one another's cup, you become One, and you become one another's strength and one another's love. As this occurs, you experience what is called enlightenment.

When you experience this alignment and attunement with the All That Is, the physical expression of your soulmate automatically appears. And if you will recognize that you already embody the principle of love, then you will merge with your soulmate and the merging of soulmates creates miracles.'

ISBN: 0 646 21150 1, size A5, 160 pages, soft cover.

GARDEN OF GODS
by Peter O. Erbe

From the author of the highly acclaimed spiritual classic 'GOD I AM', comes 'GARDEN OF GODS', a deeply inspired collection of wisdoms, presented in the form of an 'open at any page' book, which may serve as a daily companion, offering profound insights.

Excerpt: 'For ere so long have you wandered the wilderness of your own making. Deep has been the grief of your perceived separation and heavy the ache within your heart longing for home. You are the traveller who journeyed distant lands and, thirsty and spent, beholds from afar a